C000175007

TUBESOLOGY

TUBESOLOGY

THE WORLD ACCORDING TO SOCCER AM'S LEADING PUNDIT

JOHN BLAKE

Published by John Blake Publishing Ltd,
3 Bramber Court, 2 Bramber Road,
London W14 9PB, England

www.johnblakepublishing.co.uk

www.facebook.com/Johnblakepub facebook
twitter.com/johnblakepub twitter

First published in hardback in 2013

ISBN: 978-1-78219-726-3

All rights reserved. No part of this publication may be reproduced,
stored in a retrieval system, or in any form or by any means, without the
prior permission in writing of the publisher, nor be otherwise circulated
in any form of binding or cover other than that in which it is published
and without a similar condition including this condition being
imposed on the subsequent publisher.

British Library Cataloguing-in-Publication Data:

A catalogue record for this book is available from the British Library.

Design by www.envydesign.co.uk

Printed in Great Britain by CPI Group (UK) Ltd

1 3 5 7 9 10 8 6 4 2

Copyright © Peter Dale 2013

The right of Peter Dale to be identified as the Author of this Work
has been asserted by him in accordance with the Copyright,
Designs and Patents Act, 1988.

Papers used by John Blake Publishing are natural, recyclable products made
from wood grown in sustainable forests. The manufacturing processes
conform to the environmental regulations of the country of origin.

Every attempt has been made to contact the relevant copyright-holders,
but some were unobtainable. We would be grateful if the appropriate
people could contact us.

Contents

'What's Tubes like?' is the most common question I get asked. If I'm in a hurry I just reply, 'A doughnut,' but if I'm cornered or drunk I'll tell the truth. Tubes is as thick as he looks. That glorious dopey manner he portrays whilst sat in front of Sylvester Stallone, 50 Cent, or Alesha Dixon – give it up, mate! – is not the result of spending years at drama school, he just really is a match short of a fixture list. This is the guy who is convinced he can hit the undercarriage of an aeroplane with a tennis ball as it's crossing the A30 while coming in to land at Heathrow. I (bleep) you not; he thinks he can do it. I love him... LOVE YOU TUBES XXX

HELEN CHAMBERLAIN

I remember Tubes when he joined us as a chubby 16-year-old with silly hair... come to think of it not much has changed since then! I kept him on because his tea-making skills were second to none, or as he would say, 'sick'. Also him being a fellow Chelsea fan helped his cause massively! He has done all right though. Well done, mate.

TIM LOVEJOY

Like most ideas on *Soccer AM* someone, somewhere down the line, claims ownership. I think (actually I know) that I am responsible for trimming down the somewhat clunky 'Peter the Test Tube Baby' to the infinitely more user-friendly moniker of Tubes. (Should I be getting royalties? Is there a free phone number I should call?)

When Pete the work-ex unleashed that first exploding beer can onto the car park wearing a towelling nappy and vacant stare, I spat out my tea. It was so funny – so surreal and SO unexpected. Pete was (is) quiet and unassuming, and here he was 'having it' Ayia Napa – or should I say nappy? – style. You can have that. Where did it come from? Who cares, it was one of those moments etched in my *Soccer AM* memories. YouTube it.

His on-screen presence grew and he was given his now famous 'One Question and One Question Only' slot on a weekly basis. He used to tell me how nervous he was, to the point of wanting to throw up. I know how he felt – we were just lads having a laugh but getting to do it on telly. He got himself up there and did it and believe me, it is not easy.

Since then he's gone from strength to strength – interviewing some of the biggest names in football. The players love him for two reasons. Firstly, he is a genuinely nice bloke who still gets a thrill from meeting players and, secondly, he is brilliant at it. He is so natural, asks the right questions and gets great answers.

He is my mate and I'm delighted for him.

FENNERS

I have known Tubes since we were both like ten years old running around these North London estates. He wasn't from the estate though. In fact, I am not even sure if he is from North London. Come to think of it, nobody actually knew where he lived. He just kept turning up. When we all decided to become rappers and football players, although he could kick a ball unfortunately Tubes was the only one who couldn't actually make words rhyme. After some of the lads teased him he disappeared for like 15 years and then BAM! All of a sudden I saw him on *Soccer AM*! He was all over our TV screens and to our surprise he was actually rhyming!

His raps still didn't make much sense but we were still proud of him anyway, plus, he is probably more famous than all the other lads that used to laugh at his raps... except me. We are kinda like the same, I think. The others are still rapping though. They've just got nowhere to perform...

SWAY

ACKNOWLEDGEMENTS

Just wanted to thank a few people for giving me the opportunity to write the words you are about to read. First I would like to thank the big dogs at Sky for allowing me to do it. Also, a big thank you to John Blake Publishing for approaching me to do a book in the first place (although at first I did think it was a wind-up). Massive thanks to Tim Lovejoy, as if it wasn't for him, I would never been able to write this book and would still be paying off my student loan while also being about eight stone heavier. Big thanks also to my good pal Adrian Kajumba who has had a massive part in putting my weird words into proper sentences – cheers, mate.

But biggest thanks goes to all you out there, who have supported me throughout, and even put up with my budget raps for years.

TUBESOLOGY

Hope you enjoy the book, if you don't I apologise.
Keep it real,

Tubes XXX

CHAPTER 1

One Lucky (Unfit) Boy

I want to start by giving you something. I want to share with you the details of a vital secret that I have never shared with anyone before. It is only a little one (and no, before you think it, it's not an early doors Rocket gag). But it is a little tip, one that has changed my life and might well do the same for you.

Here goes...

To make the perfect cup of tea, it is essential that you let it brew for 3 minutes and 23 seconds. Add a splash of milk, give it a little stir and there you have it: the perfect Tubes Tea.

Now you are probably thinking: 'Why is he talking about tea? Shouldn't he be talking about burgers and kebabs? We've seen the shape the boy is in!' And I know, I know – you probably want to know what happened when I met

Slash from Guns N' Roses or all the details about my love affair with Alesha Dixon.

Don't worry, don't worry. We will get to those and plenty of other stories about a whole host of A-listers from the worlds of film, TV, music and sport, who have opened up after being blown away (or just completely embarrassed) by my rapping skills. But the simple cup of tea is how it all began so it is only fair it gets an early mention, especially as it is pretty amazing how far it has got me. Some of the things I have done in the last 10 years, people I have met, places I have been to, things I have seen and heard, I would never have dreamed of when I was growing up.

And I owe it all to a cuppa. My tea-making skills were pretty much all I had to offer in my early days, when I first stepped into the big wide world of work. But they helped a shy, chubby, with wrong sideburns kind of bloke plant my foot in the door at Sky.

The rest, as they say, is history – history that will be retold over the next 200 or so pages (how I have managed 200 pages I will never know) and for your entertainment... I hope!

My original life plan though, way before Tim 'Lovejoy' Lovejoy somehow managed to persuade Sky's bosses to give me job, was to be a footballer rather than to interview them. Every young boy dreams of being a professional, doing what his heroes do, and I was no different.

My big dream was to boss the midfield for Chelsea. Who knows? Maybe one day I might still get the chance. But to be honest there is probably more chance of me marrying Alesha Dixon!

ONE LUCKY (UNFIT) BOY

Another career option I considered was being a PE teacher. I just loved sport, mainly football. But then, being a teacher, you have to shout at people. I have never shouted at anyone in my life, unless it has been on a football field, so that basically ruled that option out.

In fairness, I wasn't bad at football. No honestly, I wasn't. I started kicking a ball about from a really young age – about four or five. My first team was a local one called Oxshott Royals. Life has come full circle as I am back playing for them now. I also played for all my school teams, represented my league and also my country – sorry, I meant county – Surrey, for a couple of years. Told you I wasn't too bad.

But the closest sniff I ever got to making it was when I joined non-league club Leatherhead. My manager at the time was Alex Inglethorpe, who is now the Under-21s manager at Liverpool. He was also Exeter manager when they were the non-league team that somehow got a 0–0 draw at Manchester United in the FA Cup in 2005. That result alone showed the world that Alex Inglethorpe knew a thing or two about the beautiful game. But I already knew that because he once told me I had a chance of making it as a professional footballer. He can obviously spot a player when he sees one... ha-ha.

One day he came up to me at Leatherhead's pre-season trials and said 'What are you doing here?'

At the time I thought he was having a go at me. But then he said: 'You really should be playing at a higher level. Technically, you are one of the best players I have seen. You should be at Leyton Orient or somewhere like that, at that level.'

'What do you mean?' I said.

'You've got all the ability,' he told me. 'We just need to get you fit.'

For the first time I thought 'Wow, maybe I have got a chance of making it here.'

Unfortunately the one thing I struggled with is rather important if you want to be a footballer – fitness. I just can't run to save my life. I've got zero pace. I play centre-midfield or centre-back as I have no legs so I can't go upfront and make darting runs in behind defenders. I didn't have to be a rocket scientist to realise that my inability to get out of first gear was going to seriously hamper my dreams of making it as a professional.

That didn't stop me getting compared to a Brazilian World Cup winning midfield legend, though. I once played with MC Harvey from the So Solid Crew. 'Yeah bruv, you can play, ya know,' he said. 'You are quality. You are like Dunga.' More like Jan Molby, I thought.

Actually, if I had to compare the young Tubes to anyone it would be Matt Le Tissier. I had a lovely touch and great vision just like the great man himself, who is an absolute Southampton legend. Unfortunately, I was not very light on my feet. Sorry Le Tiss!

Despite my weakness, Alex Inglethorpe still had faith in me, for some reason. He had connections too, and said he would get Leyton Orient down to come and watch me. 'In the next couple of weeks someone will be having a look at you,' I remember him telling me. That should have guaranteed that I was on my game for a little spell as he didn't say exactly when the scouts would show up. But here I am talking about it and what might have been, rather than actually doing it, so obviously something didn't work out.

Leatherhead still wanted to take me on, which was a small consolation. But by this stage I was 16 and already helping out with *Soccer AM*.

The dilemma was: either become a semi-professional footballer or go and muck around on *Soccer AM*. At school I worked quite hard but was always the kid in the class who loved mucking around. You'd never have guessed, right? I was never rude and I'd never had a fight in my life but I was always the cheeky one at the back of the class making people laugh. At least I hope I was, anyway. So choosing *Soccer AM* seemed the natural thing to do and that was the end of playing at a decent level. Now I play just for fun, mainly for the *Soccer AM* team and my beloved Oxshott Royals.

The *Soccer AM* team (then known as The Badgers) were lucky enough to play the first game ever at the new Wembley, which was an amazing experience. I marked the occasion by going for a wee in every single toilet, literally. That's something to tell the grandchildren, right? I didn't score that day but I did set up Serge 'Serge' Pizzorno from Kasabian for a good goal.

I have also recently started playing for my good mate Darren Eadie, the ex-Norwich and England midfielder, and his charity Sellebrity. We go around the country playing other teams for charity. The highlight of my foot-ball career, though, came at St Andrews in 2013, when I scored a wonder volley that bounced in off the crossbar after I flicked the ball over retired boxer Joe Calzaghe on the edge of the box.

Thinking back, it was probably a panic flick more than an intended one, because he was charging towards me as the ball dropped my way. That man is still an absolute tank. Boy, was I pleased to see somebody caught that goal on film and put it on YouTube. I would be lying if I said I haven't watched it every day since...

Another one of my greatest achievements in football is breaking the FATV record for kick-ups with a tennis ball. It is a challenge the FA run on their website and I have managed to do the most so far. I have even beaten a number of professionals, which is why I'm so proud of it.

My highest score was 195. I haven't really told many people about it – until blabbing to the world today, that is. Some of the players I have interviewed say they have seen the video and ask me if it is even real. I was speaking to Arsenal and England midfielder Alex Oxlade-Chamberlain, for one, and he could not believe it. 'What? 195? Are you serious?' he said. He got 100 and was the previous record holder. Gary Cahill, the Chelsea and England defender, says he won't believe it until I go round to his house and do it in front of him.

I went down to interview Joe Cole at West Ham and they had seen the video too. He said: 'We've got someone who can beat you!' They brought a West Ham youth player into their indoor training arena to set up the challenge... but I beat him as well. To be fair to him, he had three goes and I had five. I got 190 and he mucked it up on 170-something. He was gutted, so was I. Well, sort of... nah. Actually I wasn't at all! So I am proud to say my record still stands and it is not a bad total.

It doesn't solve the fact that I still can't run, though. I probably should have worked a bit harder when I was younger playing at Leatherhead. Jamie Mackie, who is now at Nottingham Forest, was in the year below me. I used to go down and watch him play and thought 'Yeah, this geezer is good.' Was I better than him? Hmm. He was rapid. I might have had a better touch than him, but he was the one who got spotted. But then I never really put myself out there; I'm just laid back. I was never one to go out and do extra things like jogging, and never had the 'I have got to do this if I'm going to make it' attitude. He, as an example, probably had a greater desire than me.

Once Leatherhead spelt it out that pursuing a career in football meant I would have to leave *Soccer AM* because they would need me from 1 p.m. on a Saturday, there was only one winner for me, especially as I knew I'd never make it right to the top as a player. I think it's turned out to be the right decision and things have worked out for the better. Occasionally I wonder what might have been but then I just think back to how slow I am and get a sharp slap around the face that brings me back to reality. I have seen milk turn quicker than me. Every time I go backwards, in my head I hear the horn that big lorries make when they are reversing going off!

My first job at Sky was tea boy, which is where my tea-making skills came in handy. My mum Janet is a schoolteacher and the legendary Sky commentator Martin Tyler's kids were among her pupils. She put a word in for me, got me a week of work experience at *Soccer AM* and I ended up churning out cups of tea for four years every Saturday morning.

That continued until I was a day away from going to university. I managed to get good enough A Level grades at my sixth form, St Andrews in Ashtead, Surrey, to earn a place at Canterbury Christ Church University. I did PE and got a B in that. I also did media but didn't do quite as well. I'm not even sure I should really be working for *Soccer AM*!

But then Tim Lovejoy phoned up as I was packing my bags ready to doss and get fat at uni:

'You're going tomorrow, aren't you?'

'Yeah,' I replied.

'No you're not,' he said.

'What?' I said, totally confused.

He quickly explained. 'You are not going to university. I'm getting you a job. Unpack your bags. I have just created you a job at Sky. You are the runner in the sports library, but still working with us on a Saturday!'

I just said: 'Okay.'

I had to call the uni and tell them I wasn't coming.

'What?' said the lady at the other end of the phone, who sounded thoroughly shocked and not very happy with what she had just been told. 'I'm so sorry,' I said. 'I have just got a job... ' I don't think they were best pleased.

About an hour later I got a phone call from a lady at Sky, called Pippa. 'Tim Lovejoy has just come up here and said "give Peter a job now",' she said. Of course that was my name at the time. My christening as Tubes was a few years down the line.

ONE LUCKY (UNFIT) BOY

It was the call that changed my life and a new life plan was born – literally, as it turned out. And it was all thanks to a bit of hard work, a bit of luck and, most importantly, my ability to make a world-class cup of tea.

CHAPTER 2

NAPPY RASH

I was absolutely buzzing. I was a day away from committing to three more years of written work and exams, when to be brutally honest it was never really my cup of tea and neither was I very good at it. Then, all of a sudden, I was the Sports Library Runner at Sky Sports, so a big thank you to Tim and Pippa.

Let me explain what I had to do now I had the job title 'runner'. No I didn't turn into a sprinter like Linford Christie and run around for a living. It basically meant that if there was any job that no one else wanted to do, I would have to do it. I was like a much less glamorous Claude Makalele of the office. Like Claude, nobody ever really saw what I did, but my job was vital to help keep things running smoothly.

'So and so needs this tape, go and get it Pete,' was pretty much the only thing anyone ever said to me. 'Okay, there you go,' was pretty much the only thing I ever mumbled back.

I was your typical surly teenager at the time and that little exchange counted as a revealing, deep conversation for me. I didn't even have to speak to people to do the other part of the job. If people couldn't be bothered to put tapes back where they belonged, I would go and fetch them and put them back in their rightful homes. That made me a bit like a human retriever dog, some might say. But I loved every minute of it and was so grateful to be given the chance. I still couldn't run very quick, though, and was often out of breath fetching and retrieving tapes. I really should have listened to Alex Inglethorpe a little bit more!

Eventually, life being just a runner began to get a little bit boring so I began teaching myself a few new tricks. You know all those cool TV montages that Sky chuck in during most of their programmes? They would come from someone like me, beavering away behind the scenes so someone else could have the glory of introducing a super slick, polished and pretty impressive-looking montage. Well, to start with I just helped the creative lot find the best shots. But then I started learning how to make the montages themselves – I learnt the system. That was the jargon for what I was doing. 'Being busy' is what others might call it.

My area of expertise was football, so for me it was a match made in heaven. Unsurprisingly, I loved it and at the time it seemed like a perfect job. I was basically watching football all day, every day.

I was actually starting to talk to people more too. Well, a

little bit, anyway. For example, the boys working on the various programmes covering the Premier League would come down to the sports library and say: 'We're doing a montage on Gianfranco Zola, I need his best goals, great touches, bits of skills and stuff like that.'

It was then my job to trawl the archives, find what they wanted, note down all the details, grab the tapes and hand them over. Watching Gianfranco Zola all day? Hardly a chore, is it? Especially for a Chelsea fan like me.

At the same time as I graduated to the big wide world of Sky's sports library, I started leading a double life.

One day I was doing my duties in the sports library and Tim Lovejoy called me up.

'Peter, can you come upstairs?' he said. 'We have got something for you... ' Immediately, for some reason, my first thought was 'I might get a job here.'

Upstairs I went and Tim, John 'Fenners' Fendley and Joe 'Sheephead' Worsley – the big dogs at *Soccer AM* who I had been helping out on Saturdays for a few years by this stage – were all sat around a table waiting for me.

They said: 'Little Rocket has decided to go on holiday.'

He was playing a character called Lobster Boy back in the early days of the show, where he used to dress up as a lobster (funnily enough) and bring the balls out for the end-of-show game. Oh yeah, and he'd say 'Lobster lobster fish fish'. Tim said, 'so how do you feel about being on TV as a character?'

I never thought I would be on TV, mainly because I have a face for radio and I am quite shy. When I was younger and if there were loads of people at a party I would be a bit intimidated because I didn't know anyone. I was really shy. Horribly shy.

I am still blessed, if that is the right word, with the same looks and am still shy I suppose. Now you might find that hard to believe. Especially when I have spent almost the last 10 years plucking up the courage to spit ridiculous – some would probably say poor – lyrics at some seriously big celebrities. Or going up to some of the fittest women on the planet and risking humiliation by asking them out when I've got my moobs hanging out! And in front of a TV audience of millions.

Occasionally even I step back and think 'how and why have I just done that?' The answer is, I don't know and it is a great question and probably much better than the ones I churn out every week! I suppose over the years I've just got used to doing what I have to do.

Anyhow, back to Tim Lovejoy, Fenners, Sheephead and me around a table, discussing the next move. 'How do you feel about being Peter the Test Tube Baby?' they said.

'What?' I replied, totally baffled about where that idea had come from, until they explained. 'There was an old punk rock band in the 70s and 80s called Peter and the Test Tube Babies. As you're called Peter, we think it will be funny to dress you in a nappy, have a can of beer and fake cigarette as you bring the balls out for the football game at the end of the show.'

Now you've got to bear in mind, we had this conversation in November. Winter. It was freezing. Who in their right mind would seriously want to be out in the freezing cold with just a few bits of material to protect them? The idea did not appeal to me straight away, I must admit.

I was umming and ahhing. 'You don't have to do it if you don't want to,' they said. But, after a little bit of thought, I decided it could be quite a good thing to do so I said yes.

If I'm honest I still wasn't sure exactly what to expect or what I had signed up for when I turned up to work the following Saturday. In my early days as the tea boy I used to be the one sorting out all the prop boxes so they were ready for the various characters when they got in – a bit like a kit man. Then I became Peter the Test Tube Baby and all of a sudden there was my box with my character's name on it.

'Wow. I've got a box!' I can assure you, it was a huge moment. Like my big promotion? But then I opened it, and did not like what I saw. That was the big reveal. The first time I saw the Peter the Test Tube Baby costume. It was basically what looked like a rug and a roll of gaffer tape. Also in the box was a rattle, a can of supermarket own brand beer, a fake cigarette, and then next to my box was the bag of balls. Then it finally hit me. 'What the hell am I doing?' I thought, as my heart sank.

I tried putting the rug on with absolutely no luck. You had to tuck it through your legs, under your bum and bring it around and then gaffer tape it all together. Simple, right?

I soon realised I couldn't do it all on my own so had to rope someone in to help. One of the crew came to my rescue, wrapping the gaffer tape round, and round and round and round. Then I put the dummy round my neck, grabbed the can of beer and fake cigarette and after a few more bits of fussing and fumbling I was ready.

TUBESOLOGY

I took one look in the mirror... and I realised I looked absolutely ridiculous. It felt like one big joke. A grown, hairy man in a nappy. It was also a bit weird now I think about it, especially with those documentaries that are occasionally on about adult babies. All I was waiting for was the late Jeremy Beadle to jump out and go, 'Ahhhhhhhhhhhhhh got you, you mug'. But Jeremy Beadle was nowhere to be seen. There was no escape. This was the real thing.

When my big screen debut arrived the last-minute instructions from the backroom team were simple. 'Get the can of beer, shake that up and when Helen Chamberlain says the words 'Peter the Test Tube Baby' and the music comes on that's your cue to just walk on with the balls, give them to Helen, open the can, do a little dance and walk off.'

There really was no escape by this stage. It was way too late. So I decided to just have a laugh with it.

My time came. The music started, I shook the beer, opened it, hit myself on the head – which really hurt, though I think I managed to hide it – and I did what I had to do! And Peter the Test Tube Baby became a regular feature

Sure enough, it soon felt like second nature. Go on national TV and act a bit stupid for a few minutes. For a kid who loved mucking around in school, it was not like I had to change too much to do it. I got really into the act too, throwing in roly polys and all sorts. There were a few downsides. I nearly got injured a fair few times and being exposed to the elements with just a bit of material to cover my crown jewels meant there also a number of times when it felt like I was quite close to pneumonia too. It may sound daft, but I loved it.

My stupid antics in a nappy had also started to get me noticed. I was still working in the sports library during the week, logging sports news and generally finding football clips, but then parading round on a Saturday as a big fat, full-grown hairy baby. People around Sky would look at me like a freak and say, 'Are you Peter the Test Tube Baby? I'm sure I saw you on TV dressed in a nappy.' It was so weird, and there was no point in trying to deny it was me, because the sideburns I had at the time made me instantly recognisable (because they looked awful – nobody else would degrade themselves with those beauts!) Now I realise why I didn't cuddle a girl over the sideburn years...

I started getting noticed for the first time outside of work too. Now that really used to freak me out, something to this day I still find rather bizarre. Remember, I started out as just a shy kid from the mean streets of Cobham, in Surrey, who was best known for making tea and being really unfit. Becoming a character on a TV show with a regular slot was hard enough to get my head around. Yet the more I kept doing it, the more I would have people coming up to me, staring at me in disbelief before asking, 'Are you that bloke from *Soccer AM*?' And, without meaning to sound like Charlie Big Spuds, it got to a stage where pretty much most places I went to, there would always be at least one random person who would greet me by shouting 'Tuuuuuuuuuuuuubes' in my direction.

I will never forget the first time it happened. I was having a drink in Epsom and a girl came up to me and asked: 'Are you Peter the Test Tube Baby?' I thought: 'What? Wow. Someone has just recognised me.' I thought someone was winding me up. My mate just laughed and said: 'You're famous now!' I was like, "Shut up mate, it's all a big wind-up."

When I go to Chelsea games I often get people recognising me and start doing the song from the old Peter the Test Tube Baby sketch, or saying, 'Oi Tubes, do me one of those rubbish raps.' I still have to pinch myself. For me it's really weird.

It still seems strange because people are so nice to me, something that I'm very thankful for (so thank you). You could get a lot of stick as a result of what I do. I know if I was watching some of the nonsense I come out with, I'd want to give me a bit of stick. I suppose it's because I just roll up and do what I've got to do. It's clearly just a bit of harmless fun.

I genuinely hope that is how it comes across, because that is all it is supposed to be. I'm not trying to come across as a proper presenter speaking in a posh newsreader accent, though that's mainly due to the fact that when you are brought up living in the ghetto of Cobham your vocab ain't ever gonna be all dat you get me?

It's all very relaxed on *Soccer AM* and I would say that has really helped us get some of the interviews we have. I think the people I interview realise I'm not there to stitch anyone up, or get a story into the paper. I'm just there to have a laugh really.

When we went to see Real Madrid star Gareth Bale last season when he was at Tottenham, he was turning down interviews with a number of media. But he was more than happy to do a bit for *Soccer AM* because he knew it would be a laugh. That's exactly how it turned out and we ended up talking about him being an underwear bandit with Arsenal speed merchant Theo Walcott when they were youth teamers at Southampton. Don't worry, it's not as bad as it sounds. It was all just innocent fun. But more on that in Chapter 16.

Back in the days of Peter the Test Tube Baby, the idea of rubbing shoulders with the Premier League's best footballers never entered my head. I was still just trying to make a success of my act. We started introducing sketches during the show when I had to play other characters, which took me even further out of my comfort zone. I am cringing and squirming thinking about some of them now.

The acting bit was not me. Like football and not being able to run, I could not speak – on camera obviously – and I could not act. None of the crew were actors, but most of them were much, much better than me (though that wasn't really hard, trust me).

Fenners could act, in fact he was brilliant. The guy is a genius, someone who I looked up to when I was the tea boy learning the ropes and who I still go to for advice now, and have been fortunate to work alongside with on different projects. My favourite characters of his were Stan Hibbert and Barry Proudfoot, but to be honest anything he did was pretty good value.

Fenners has had a big part to play in the success of *Soccer AM*. He is one of the funniest guys I've ever met. He creases me up. He writes all the ideas for sketches and characters himself and his passion is unbelievable.

Sometimes he used to come up with ideas that made you think, 'Where on earth did that come from?!'

Together Fenners and Sheephead were absolute geniuses. When they used to do sketches they would deliver hilarious punchline after hilarious punchline after hilarious punchline. There was no need for an autocue with those two about.

Their accents and voices were a different class too. Fenners can do any voice. His impression of the late Nottingham Forest manager Brian Clough is up there. He's a perfectionist too, which is probably part of the reason why he's so good. If he is trying to nail a voice or accent he'll do it again and again and again until it is absolutely perfect.

Sometimes when you are filming a sketch like Barry Proudfoot and you're starting at 7 a.m. and finishing at midday, it's not always ideal. Everyone would say, 'Come on Fenners!'

But he wouldn't care. 'I can do that better, I know I can do that better,' he'd say. There was no stopping him until it was spot on. He is brilliant. And he has given me loads of advice too. One of the best was pretty simple – just stick with it and keep going. For four years he kept telling me to keep going, keep going, keep going, just be yourself and you will get the rewards.

Fenners certainly never stops. He is persistent. Like a little kid. Like that time he accidentally punched Tim in the face by accident when he and Sheephead were doing a sketch dressed as Aussie Rules footballers and after every gag pretending to attack each other with fake punches and headbutts. Because he is persistent, he just got caught up in the moment of the sketch and accidentally laid one on Tim. He was still in character. Tim was on the floor in the pain and everyone else was in tears of laughter. Fenners just carried on because he was in character but you could see on his face he was starting to panic about lamping his boss.

As well as being a creative genius, Fenners was also the top prankster on the show. Just ahead of Sheephead, who was seriously funny too. He's got a proper dry sense of humour and is a lovely man.

There are too many funny Fenners stories to tell but one sticks out. We used to have Polaroid cameras that were supposed to be used to take pictures of the guests when they were backstage. Just to repeat that, they were for the guests. But the little kid in Fenners just couldn't help taking what are best described as inappropriate photos, normally of himself and Sheephead, and then use them to try and distract Tim Lovejoy. When they would come out to do their various sketches they'd discreetly pass the pictures to Lovejoy or plant them somewhere he'd see, like on his clipboard with his notes. But you at home wouldn't have a clue that anything was going on.

They loved trying to see if they could put Lovejoy off during the show, while it was live, and see if he could keep his composure while all these pranks were going on. They would come on and just quickly slip a picture in somewhere, and then just walk off set as if nothing has happened and watch him try not to crack up. It wasn't every week so Tim never knew when the joke was coming. It was probably once a month. It was hilarious. So many times Tim used to fail to hold it in but you'd never really know what he was laughing at – he obviously couldn't point it out on live TV!

Fenners loved an inappropriate joke too, but they were so good you had to be wide awake to make sure you got them too. Once Gavin Henson, who was then going out with Welsh singer Charlotte Church, was on the show, and in one of his sketches Fenners was pretending to be an army soldier, talking to another soldier via a walkie-talkie. He said: 'Charlotte Church... Charlotte Church, over.' Then he pretended that the other soldier replied to him over the walkie-talkie and said: 'Yep. Roger that.' Gavin Henson's face was a picture. He was not impressed to say the least. The smile fell off his face instantly

Although I wasn't anywhere near Fenners' level of acting ability, I threw myself into it all the same and ended up getting more roles while I was still playing Peter the Test Tube Baby at the end of the show. Things were really kicking off by this stage and it got to the point where I was needed for every show.

But eventually Peter the Test Tube Baby act had run its course. It was time to move on. After three years everyone thought it was still funny, but it was getting tired.

Tim had had enough of seeing me naked except for a makeshift nappy, come out with a basket of balls, dance around for a bit, spray my beer, chuck it in my face, lob the can away and give Helen the balls for the game. 'You've had three years of it, it's done now,' was his final assessment of a character I had nurtured and grown to love. Actually, not love, just get used to.

But there was more. 'I think you'll be good on camera,'

he continued. At this point I was thinking: 'Is this some kind of sick joke?' But then he said: 'You've got one question and one question only.'

CHAPTER 3

ONE QUESTION AND ONE QUESTION ONLY: IS HE FOR REAL?

A s you've probably guessed, I got on really well with Tim Lovejoy. I think it was purely down to the Chelsea connection – lifelong supporters through the bad and good times and due to that alone our bromance started.

You can imagine the conversation:

'Who do you support?'

'Chelsea.'

'So do I. Get in.'

And from there we became good friends and often used to go down to Chelsea together straight after the show on a Saturday morning.

How would I describe him having got to know him? Quite simply, as a nice man. A top bloke. Everyone knew he was the boss, but he was one of the boys often getting right amongst the madness of the *Soccer AM* office. Nobody really took the mickey out of him because he did it himself and that's what I liked about him. I do the same so that is probably another big reason why we got on so well.

All the 'Lovejoy is a Legend' stuff and telling people he'd send them a fiver if they could get a banner or sign with 'Lovejoy is a Legend' on TV was just a big joke. He really laughs at himself.

But he is a genius. He started at *The Big Breakfast* under Chris Evans before joining Sky as part of the production team, and then decided he wanted to produce and present *Soccer AM*. So the story goes – and I'm pretty sure he didn't just make this up to make himself look good – back in the day he just went up to one of the big bosses at Sky and said: 'I will make this show great.' They said, 'Go on then,' and he only went and did it, didn't he! He wasn't a bad footballer either, but he couldn't take a penalty to save his life. I think he once hit one for The Badgers that ended up somewhere in the next town. Apart from that you'll never hear a bad word from me about Tim after all he has done for me.

For starters you wouldn't be reading this book (if you're still reading it) if it wasn't for him – I probably wouldn't have done anything worth writing about. In fact, I could make a pretty good guess at how different my life might have been. At one stage I would definitely have been a fat student if it wasn't for his intervention. Who knows what would have happened after that and how things might have turned out.

True, I put in the graft for four years, but without a massive leg-up or five from Tim I would not be doing what I'm doing today. I put it solely down to him. Cheers mate.

However, enough of the soppy stuff. Because I did have real reason to question how well he actually knew me when he unveiled his latest grand plan – to get me to actually speak. On camera, no script. Also with no instructions.

It was during the summer break that he phoned me up. I was in the garden doing kick-ups and he said: 'Right, next year. You've got one question and one question only. Do what you want.'

And then put the phone down. I had to phone him back up. I mean what the hell did that mean? 'Yep,' he said. 'You come on, ask one question and then you go off.' 'What do I ask?' I said. It was like trying to get blood out of a stone. 'It's up to you,' he said. 'But you've only got three chances.'

The acting as Peter the Test Tube Baby and other sketches was OK. I could just about handle that. I either had no words to say or just had a few scripted things I needed to learn. This asking guests a question thing was a whole new kettle of fish, and it made me wonder whether he actually knew me at all. I might make people laugh in the office when it was just us about, but strangers, icons, celebrities – would it work with them?

One thing I did which had people in stitches was the sausage challenge with Robbie 'The Tramp' Knox. The Tramp was one of the weirdest and funniest blokes I have ever met. His randomness was summed up pretty well the day he asked me, totally out of the blue, if I liked sausages.

'Yeah, I like sausages,' I said. 'Actually I love them.'

'How much do you love them?' he said.

'Okay,' he said, 'let's see how much you love sausages.'

Off he went up to the canteen and he came back down with five sausages for me, which I had to finish by the end of the day.

The following Wednesday we had the same conversation. This time it was his turn to do the challenge. Up to the canteen I went and I bought him six sausages to eat, again, by the end of the day. This continued every week, every Wednesday, as we took it in turns to prove we were up to the challenge of eating however many sausages were put in front of us.

I remember the day The Tramp came down with 20 sausages for me to eat. They were bursting out of the container he was given them in. He plonked them down in front of me, looking all satisfied. 'There you go,' he said, with a big smile on his face. 'You have to finish them.' With 20 sausages to get through, there was no point in me having lunch that day. The next week I went and got him 25. Take that Tramp!

The challenge only stopped when he left *Soccer AM*. I have no idea who won. There are probably still sausages on the floor in our office somewhere.

I still love sausages too, despite being basically forcefed them by The Tramp. Especially those cheap ones you get in the cafes, of course, topped off with a little bit of no-name, cheap ketchup. Cheers Tramp!

That challenge was totally random, but a bit of a laugh. I was OK doing silly things like that and acting stupid for a giggle with friends and colleagues. But putting me on camera was a potential serious error. There was every chance it would end with a car crash TV moment. Come to think of it that may have been Tim's plan, as it was for most weeks!

As for the 'One Question and One Question Only' idea, to this day I have no clue where he plucked that from. It felt like it came from nowhere. His explanation of the idea he had in his head was terrible too, to put it bluntly

In fact it wasn't terrible, rather pretty much non-existent. To this day I have no idea if what I do matches with his original vision. 'Just pick whoever you want and ask them one question. You've got three attempts, and if after then you're still pants, you're a goner son!' Not a single proper instruction. That is unless you consider, 'Do what you want, say what you want,' as instructions. I didn't.

There was no warm-up or run-through in the week leading up to the show either.

It was going live first time. I was either to sink or swim. Or should that be totally bomb. All week, I couldn't sleep. The thought of it all just gave me cold sweats.

Frank Worthington, who had played about a million games for a million different clubs in this country, represented England and was also a bit of a playboy in his day, was a guest on the show, and I decided he was going to be my first victim.

'What should I ask Frank Worthington on the show?' I cried down the phone to my mum, my dad, my nan, my second cousin twice removed – basically anyone who would pick it up. I pestered everyone all week.

Unsurprisingly, the first attempt at Tim's brilliant new idea was actually terrible. In the absence of any advice from him, the one thing I kept reminding myself was, 'Don't try to be funny because to be honest you aren't that funny.' As strange as it sounds that is a key thing with TV – when you try too hard to be funny you tend to just fall flat on your face. Other than that, I didn't know what I was doing, so when my time came, I just went for it.

Tim did not help. He was cracking up when I shuffled out awkwardly and bricking it into the studio and onto the platform where the famous *Soccer AM* sofas are for the debut of my new slot. 'You all right?' he asked, while failing badly to hide his laughter. 'Yeah... ' It was all I could manage.

My hand was shaking furiously. Tim was still cracking up. I am sure he was actually laughing harder and harder as time went on. I was petrified and he was not helping one bit. I did a quick scan of the studio and could see everyone thinking, 'Oh my God, what is going to happen here? It's going to be horrendous.' I felt the same. I had hardly slept all week, literally, because I was so nervous.

'Who is your question for?' Tim asked. 'It's for Frank,' I said. As they still do now, the lights went down and a spotlight shone on Frank Worthington. The time had come. Everything I was building up to for the whole week. I felt like I was going to pass out.

'Alwight Frank?' I said.

'All right,' he said back.

Here goes. 'Did you score more on the pitch or off the pitch?'

'On,' he said.

I let out an awkward 'Okay, thanks,' and walked off. Actually, I might have sprinted I was so desperate to get out of there.

ONE QUESTION AND ONE QUESTION ONLY: IS HE FOR REAL?

It was not picked up on the cameras, but Tim looked at me as if to say: 'What the hell was that? That was awful! You're gonna have to do a whole lot better next week.' It was supposed to be a funny addition to the show. It wasn't. Watching it back it just looked a little confusing. I was just relieved it was all over. For a week anyway.

During the following week everyone was saying to me, 'That was poor,' and 'You looked like a mess!' Firstly, that was really helpful and kind of them... not. Secondly, that's because I was a mess!

I was still feeling pretty bad and nervous leading up to my second attempt at Tim's 'brilliant' idea for a new slot on the show. But because I had done it and just about got through it by the skin of my teeth the week before I still thought: 'Right, I can give this another go.' I was not defeated just yet.

This week leading up to attempt number two was also when my career as a rapper began, thanks to an unlikely inspiration.

I used to go to school in Ashtead. It's an area like Cobham where you have to watch your back at all times... not. It still had some of the same issues as other areas up and down the country, though, one of those being the groups of white kids who swagger around talking a little bit like they are gangsters. You know the ones... 'Wha' you saying bruva?', 'That was blatantly sick ya know' or 'I'm gonna box you like a soldier,' is normally how they start a conversation. Yeah, those kids.

I used to see them around Ashtead all the time. In fact I'm not sure there was ever a time when I was at the train station and one of these kids didn't come up to me and say, 'Bruv, give me a nugget!' At first I thought they were talking about a chicken nugget and wondered why they expected me to be walking around with one in my pocket. It took me a little while to realise they were talking about a pound coin.

I am from Surrey. I had no idea what they were talking about or when a pound coin became a nugget. I was mates with them, but it still amused me when they used to come up to me and say, 'Wha' you saying?' I would always just answer literally: 'What am I saying? Nothing. You?'

Despite giving them an answer, they would still just repeat themselves: 'So, so, so wha' you saying?' I was thinking: 'What am I saying? I just answered that question a second ago. What do they want me to say?' Me and Fenners, to this day, still greet each other like that, in what has now become a regular tribute to Ashtead's gangster wannabes.

These kids, as poor as their conversational skills were, led to my big light bulb moment. I thought 'this could be something I could incorporate into my One Question and One Question Only... ' It was a big risk. But it couldn't be any worse than the week before with Frank Worthington.

The following week (my second chance) Phil 'the Power' Taylor was the target of the question. With more of an idea about what I was getting into, I felt more prepared. Especially with my secret rapping weapon up my sleeve.

'You all right Tubes? You got a second question this week?' Helen and Tim said.

'Yeah. It's for... Phil

I was still a bit nervous but I just went in for it... 'Ruff it up rudeboy, you're coming on SICK ya know!!!'

Everyone's jaws dropped. The guests were creasing up. The reaction was perfect and I thought... 'I think I've done all right here.'

The question was a tame one. Something about throwing darts at someone or something like that. But the truth was it didn't matter. After the low of the previous week I was buzzing. I had nailed it, but mind you that was not exactly hard after the cringe fest the week before. Later on Tim came up to me and said: 'That's much better mate. The feature stays.' He was probably as happy as I was because it was his idea.

From that point on I became known as a comedy rapper. Well, a bad comedy rapper. Like with Peter the Test Tube Baby I started to get braver and adding new bits to the act, like that ridiculous noise I make with my mouth and cheeks. From this point, it will be referred to as the cheek wobble. It is so odd you can't even actually put it or what it sounds like into words. I could always do that when I was younger so decided to sling that in as well.

It tends to go down a storm too, especially when ex-footballer Neil 'Razor' Ruddock, ex-boxer Ricky 'The Hitman' Hatton or the actor Stephen Graham are on the show. When I did that noise for the first time to Razor and The Hitman I had never seen two people laugh so much in my whole life. Obviously Neil Ruddock is what I would call 'out there' anyway. Big, brash, loud and extrovert. So I am sure you can imagine how loud and hard he was laughing. 'What on earth is that? What is that, what is that,' he kept saying in that high-pitched voice of his when he's laughing.

Ricky Hatton's reaction was similar – but with a few swear words thrown in! Also Stephen Graham, who is a top-notch actor by the way, always helps me out by laughing with me. Actually, it could be at me.

The main thing was Tim liked it and so, it seemed, did the people who watch the show, hence why I am still getting wheeled out every Saturday eight years later. These days it just comes to me straight away. I listen to the interviews that Helen and now Max Rushden do with the guests on the sofa and the question I want to ask comes to me pretty quickly.

It would be wrong of me to take all the credit though. So I have to thank all those strange kids I grew up with in Ashtead for inspiring me. Next time I see you, I will spare you a nugget. Safe innit.

CHAPTER 4

IS THIS REALLY HAPPENING?

The simple ideas are often the best ones. I think that is why Tim Lovejoy's One Question and One Question Only idea worked so well.

It was like a pop-up slot for the show. I could be anywhere doing any interview and I could throw it in and potentially get some gold dust. So then we decided to take it out of the studio and onto the road.

But it wasn't like I was given a gentle introduction. First up was film hardman Ray Winstone, ironically at the Grosvenor Hotel. 'Grosvenor Friday you'll be there, yes yes yes yes yes yes, no no no no no.' Ha-ha. *Sexy Beast*! I love that Ray Winstone film!

The nerves kicked in again for two reasons. Firstly because, having got used to grilling studio guests with the type of incisive questions Jeremy Paxman would proud of,

I was kicked out of my comfort zone again. It was all change. Secondly, Ray Winstone was hard. He could probably crush me with two fingers if I rubbed him up the wrong way.

One thing in my favour was he had been on the show before so he at least recognised me when I turned up. I quickly discovered that counted for little though.

'Alwight son, alwight mate,' he said, in his thick, 'I'm a hardman who can crush you with two fingers' East London accent.

'Hi Ray, I'm Tubes from *Soccer AM*. I've got One Question and One Question Only.'

Giving me an answer turned out to be the least of his concerns. 'You what? You flipping wasting my time?'

'Eh?' I thought. That was not the reaction I had expected. Everyone knew what the One Question and One Question Only was all about by now so why did he flip out.

I was a little scared. Ray Winstone was not somebody to mess about with so I just played dumb. 'Er, er, what?' I stuttered.

'You've brought me down here to just ask me one question?' he growled back. 'Because I could be seeing my daughters. You're wasting my time.'

To be fair he had a point. Have you seen his daughter Jaime Winstone lately? HELLOOO.

Anyhow, we had gone all the way to Grosvenor Hotel and turned up mob-handed, setting up two cameras, to ask just one question. For me that is the beauty of One Question and One Question Only. But I have lost count of the amount of people who are left genuinely baffled by the idea. 'Is that it?' they ask. 'Yep. All done. Cheers. See ya.' Off we go, while they are left totally confused.

I didn't know if Ray Winstone was being serious or not, but I definitely knew I was bricking it. 'No. I've just only got one question. I think that's enough,' I insisted. It was all I was brave enough to mumble back.

'Well it's not, is it?' he barked, looking like he is getting angrier by the second.

I couldn't work it out. I was thinking 'I'm going to get it now.' I was getting ready to do a runner and must've had a look of sheer terror on my face when finally he cracked. Thankfully.

'Ahhhhhh, I got you, you mug,' he said, as he burst out laughing.

Once my heart rate got back down to somewhere like normal and I stopped sweating, I realised that was quite a good lesson from Ray Winstone. But Raymundo let me tell you something... you were so close to getting a dry slap!

Before that interview, I always took everything and every answer from every celebrity so seriously. But Ray Winstone taught me not only can playing dumb get me out of a sticky situation, it also comes across quite funny on TV.

I would say that was the case in one of the most memorable interviews I did, with the legend that is Denzel Washington. Whenever I have interviewed film stars, they tend to be at what is known in the industry as film junkets, which are usually held at plush hotels like The Dorchester or the Soho Hotel in London. All the stars from the film are all set up in different rooms ready and waiting to be interviewed. Meanwhile, the journalists (and me) are held in a waiting room until it's your turn to speak to whichever actor or actress you are going to interview about the film. They plug the film, you get your time with your whoever the actor or actress is. You're supposed to talk about the film. But I always end up finding something else random to talk about instead.

I also find the pre-interview scenario funny. It is all very pretentious. You walk into the waiting room and there will be interviewers from other shows already there.

You can hear them muttering away in their put on, super posh voices, speaking the Queen's English and wearing their best clothes. It is pretty clear they take themselves very seriously.

Meanwhile I roll in with an old pair of jeans on, a black shirt from George at Asda that is often straight out of the packet so it still has crease lines all over the garment, and just sit in the corner chilling out.

If you ask me generally many of these journalists just talk nonsense. They're the type who actually manage to convince themselves they know these Hollywood stars. They all sit around talking about the films like cinema experts. Occasionally you hear them drop in a sentence that starts something like, 'Last time I saw Den... ' when they're talking about Denzel Washington, for example. It's hilarious. The chances are he doesn't even have the slightest clue who they are. Yes they might have interviewed him seven or eight times and said hello, but in their heads, this means that they've become best friends.

I don't get involved in that. I just sit there in that corner playing Snake on my phone, minding my own business. I tend to bump into the same old faces at the junkets and they always look absolutely delighted to see me... not! The truth is they can barely bring themselves to look at me when I walk through the door. I am lucky if I get a totally unenthusiastic 'All right?' from them while they are looking the other way. They could not be less interested in me if they tried.

When I turned up for the Denzel Washington junket ahead of his film *Unstoppable*, one of the journalists did not appear to be the sharpest tool in the box. 'Are you doing Denzel Washington today?' he asked.

'No,' I said. 'I just thought I'd come and sit in the room and eat some overpriced sandwiches [with the crusts cut off – what is that all about by the way?] for a laugh.'

'What?' he said, clearly not grasping the concept of sarcasm.

'Of course I'm here to speak to Denzel Washington,' I said, spelling it out for him.

'Oh. Good luck,' he said.

'What do you mean?' I asked.

'He'll hate you,' he said.

'Really? No change there then,' I said. 'That will be great for TV.'

'No, he really, really won't like you,' he insisted.

'Okay, this sounds like it's going to be fun.'

I could tell he was totally confused about why his attempt at a warning had clearly gone in one ear and straight out of the other and I sounded quite pleased that Denzel Washington might hate me. He claimed that Denzel Washington didn't like people messing around in his interviews. I wasn't going to let that change the way I was though – I'm a rapper for life, you get me?

So I went in there and pretty much the first thing I did was warm up by rapping at Denzel Washington. 'Hi Denzel, I'm Tubes from *Soccer AM*. I've got One Question and One Question Only.'

'You're a top man, you are Den, I have been rapping since I was ten... rapping's for life, not just for Christmas... lyric overload.'

He seemed to take it well and was smiling so I started waffling some rubbish at him. Then the smile quickly fell off his face and he finally broke his silence. 'What did you say?' he shouted at me. I was startled. My eyes almost popped out of my head. He caught me totally off guard. And it was not going to be the first time I felt like that.

My first thought was what the guy had told me in the room before, that Denzel Washington would not be a fan of my messing about. It seemed like he was spot on. I didn't know whether he was acting or not. It was impossible to tell. And half of the fun of doing the interviews is not knowing how people are going to react. Denzel Washington being upset before I had even asked my question was not what I had in mind, though, so I tried again.

> Tubes: I love you mate. You are one of my
> favourite actors.
> Denzel Washington: Don't talk to me.
> T: Huh?
> DW: Don't talk to me. Don't ask me any
> questions. I don't want to talk to you.

T: Chillax.
DW: Get out.

I was getting close to accepting that the guy was right with his warning. Still, I thought I would keep up playing dumb and see where it got me.

T: I love you.

Finally I broke him, as he started cracking up.

DW: You are sick. A sick young man.
T: No I'm not.
DW: Where you from?
T: Cobham.
DW: Live with your parents.
T: No.
DW: You haven't got parents?
T: No, I have got parents.
DW: What would your mum and dad say right now?
T: Probably 'Wow, you're meeting big Den!'

He was in stitches by this stage and I knew I had got him. He was broken for good. From there the whole conversation just descended into what I could only describe as two minutes of absolute nonsense. To the point where Denzel Washington claimed he too is a rapper – just like me – and has written lyrics for some of the biggest names in the game like Jay Z, Nas and Notorious B.I.G, but if he gave any lyrics to me he would have to kill me. Told you it was nonsense!

And there was more to come as we started firing answers back at each other so quickly it was like we were competing against each other.

> T: You are such a cool man.
> DW: Yes. Yes I am.
> T: Anyway, my question is...
> DW: I don't care what your question is.
> T: Oh come on. Just one question...
> DW: Did I say you could talk?
> T: No.
> DW: Then shut up. Just do what I tell you to do. You understand?
> T: Yes sir.
> DW: Well ask me a question then.
> T: OK... Wh...
> DW: NO!
> T: You are better than I thought you would be.

Cue more laughter.

> DW: Yes I am. I am 'Unstoppable'. [A well-worked in plug to please the junket organisers!]
> T: Can I ask you a question now?
> DW: Yes you can.
> T: Thank you.
> DW: You are welcome.
> T: What makes you happy?

DW: Interviews. Interviews with rappers.

T: You get me, bruv.

DW: Peace.

T: Is that it?

DW: One.

T: Two.

DW: 100.

T: 100?

DW: You know what that means?

T: No.

DW: That means complete. 100. Outy. You know what that means?

T: Is that American?

DW: Yeah outy. You know what outy means?

T: Audi?

DW: Yeah 'outy' like I'm outta here.

T: Oh, outy? That's 'howdy'. Audi is the car

DW: It means I'm gone.

T: What makes you happy?

Denzel Washington's response was silence. Just silence.

T: Not much then I take it.

Still more silence from Big Den.

T: I love you man.

DW: Never change. You are the best. That's how you got here. That's why you are leaving.

T: What a legend.

And with that, I got up and walked out.

By this point it was clear he was mucking around for most of the interview and once the cameras went off and we stopped filming he just grabbed me and gave me a massive hug.

'That was brilliant,' he said, with a huge smile on his face. 'Make sure you come back to all my junkets.'

He told his entourage he wanted me back too because he gets bored of talking about the same stuff all the time.

'How do you come up with all that?' he said. 'It's just a laugh, isn't it?' was my simple explanation. 'That's exactly what it is and should be: a laugh,' he said. 'So that's why I want you to come back. I get bored. I have to answer the same answers but in a different way to the same interviewer from each channel.'

That was great to hear.

Leonardo DiCaprio and Colin Farrell are two others who have said the same about wanting me to go back. I must admit that sounds weird to say such a thing so casually. Every time I interview Colin Farrell he specifically and genuinely asks for me to be put in the middle of his running order of interviews because the chance to mess about breaks up the day for him.

Don't get me wrong though. There are plenty of people who never ever want to see my face again – Jessica Alba, Steve Coogan, half my family, to name but a few.

Denzel Washington was not finished with the invite back, though. He had one more surprise. After playing tricks with me he wanted to play one on the rest of the journalists in the waiting room. Just as I was about to leave, he opened the hotel room door for me, but rather than just send me on my way he grabbed and shoved me into headlock before dragging me through the corridor, past all the people in the waiting room.

I could just about turn my neck to catch a glimpse of all the other interviewers waiting for their turn to go and see Big Den. They were all sat there... stunned. Their jaws were on the floor as Denzel Washington hauled me through the corridors shouting 'Don't mess with Big Den, Tuuuubes. Don't mess with Big Den.'

Nobody's face was more of a picture than the guy who had warned me about Denzel Washington beforehand. I could see he was in total disbelief. I walked back into the waiting room, picked up my tapes and left. The look on his face was priceless. Denzel Washington is one of my favourite actors, so when the journalist had said he'd hate me it wasn't really what I wanted to hear. All I was hoping was that if he was someone who changed from day to day that I would get him on a good day. It seemed I did. Having said that, I haven't been back to one of his junkets yet!

That was a pretty impressive offer from Denzel Washington. It is up there with one I got from Jean-Claude Van Damme, when he asked me to star in a film alongside him. Jean-Claude is a bit of a hero of mine; I used to love all his fighting scenes in films when I was growing up. For some reason, when I got to his junket for the film *The Expendables 2* I thought he was going to be weird. I can't put my finger on why I thought that. It was just a hunch.

The pre-interview warnings from the others in the waiting room put me on edge again too, doubting whether he would take to me or not. It was like Denzel Washington all over again.

First I had to speak to Dolph Lundgren, who was also in the film. We had met a couple of years before at the first *Expendables* film junket and, basically, he didn't like me because he didn't really understand what was going on. He was obviously used to doing sit-down interviews in a certain way, then I came in out of nowhere and he clearly thought: 'What the hell is this geezer doing rapping and staring at me like a weirdo?'

Just when it was starting to get awkward I managed to claw the situation back by saying something that made him laugh which broke the ice and made him realise I wasn't taking the mickey, but actually just having a laugh.

Before that icebreaker it was getting pretty tense in that hotel room though. Having Dolph Lundgren, who is an absolute unit by the way, looking at you like he is about to tear your head off is not a position I would recommend any-one getting themselves in to. Whenever I have seen him since though he has pretty much cheered me into the room and been delighted to see me. This time I walked in and straight away his face lit up as if to say 'yeah, I'm ready for you this time.' It was quite funny because we started talking about random things like my ears – he said I had ears like Spock from *Star Trek*, and even though it was a bit bizarre it was just good taste of things to come.

That was my warm-up and I came out buzzing a bit, ready to take on Jean-Claude Van Damme.

When I walked in I had a feeling that what was about to unfold was going to end up being funny and he would be a bit weird, a bit of a nutcase. I think it was mainly because of the funny beer TV adverts that he was also in at the time – I mean, you have to be a little bit off the wall to be a grown man doing snow angels in a TV advert.

But he didn't know what a *Soccer AM* interview was all about. So when I walked into the room and he was staring back at me with a serious, stern look on his face I was fearing the worst. A quick demonstration of his snow angels got him into the spirit though, and it finally did turn into the random interview I was expecting. It all began with a question about Royal Rumble:

Tubes: Hi Jean-Claude I'm Tubes from *Soccer AM*. I've got One Question and One Question Only. You're a top man, you are Van Damme, I'm really fat (rip open shirt and shake my moobs) and I hate my spam, oooooh I hate my spam.

Jean-Claude Van Damme: That's good. That is a good one. I did a similar one in a beer commercial when I open the shirt and you can see my nipples and they are hard like they are frozen because of the snow on top of the mountain.

T: The ones with the snow angel?

VD: Yes, yes, you saw it?

T: Yeah. I'm in better shape though, right?

VD: Yeah, you are hairy. Women love that.

T: You're a top bloke and I love you. You are one of my favourite actors.

VD: Thank you.

T: But if all the cast were going to have Royal Rumble, who would win a fight out of all the cast of *The Expendables*?

VD: Who would win? I don't know. I run so fast by the time I am over there, they will still be over there behind me destroying each other and there will probably be another movie. I am not a fighter, I am a lover.

He didn't even answer the question properly in the end but jumped at the chance to perform a fight move on me. And sure enough it wasn't long before we were fake fighting just like they do in the films, complete with sound effects. Crack, slap, whip. It was completely bizarre. Mental, as we pretended to slap and punch each other.

If I'd had the time, I would've been pinching myself. I was sat there, with my shirt still ripped open having a play fight with film legend Jean-Claude Van Damme. It was such a weird situation. One I could never ever have imagined being in. He is a funny guy and a bit mental. I have always got to be aware of what might come next – there was no time to sit there going: 'Wow, this is mad, what am I doing?' I've got to be alert and ready to react to whatever is thrown at me – in this case, literally. I must admit though, it was pretty hard to keep that level-headedness while I was play fighting with Jean-Claude Van Damme!

At the end he was really nice and said: 'That is proper television.' 'Really?' I thought. 'We were just being silly and fought each other.' 'No, that is proper television. It really is,' he said.

Then just as I got up to leave he told me: 'I want to work with you.' 'Seriously?' I thought. The day just got even more bizarre.

Just to make sure I got the message, one of his entourage walked after me after I left the room and said: 'Here is Jean's card. He wants you to email him because he likes you.'

Stupidly, I have lost the card and I didn't follow it up. Maybe I should have. How cool would that be, to work with Jean-Claude Van Damme? I have no idea what we would do. Snow angels? A film maybe?

I wouldn't mind appearing in a film. I reckon I would only be good at playing myself, a dopey kind of character. Who knows whether I'd be any good – actually, no, I probably wouldn't. But I'd love to give it a go though. So Jean, if you happen to be reading this (there is probably more chance of me having kids with Alesha Dixon!) please get in touch! And sorry for losing your business card.

Another tempting offer I have received but not cashed in was an invite for a night out with Colin Farrell. The first time I interviewed him, ahead of his film *London Boulevard*, I wasn't sure what to expect. I'd heard some stories about a powerful personality. And I had the potential to provoke him.

But he was such a cool guy. I asked him what the naughtiest thing he has ever done was. He was struggling for ideas so I told him I once nicked a cola bottle from a corner shop. Then we ended up talking about Garbage Pail Kid stickers and how his failure to successfully nick a packet from a shop proved he would never make it as a criminal and turned him towards acting. Just to be clear, he was mucking around about ever wanting to be a criminal!

Before we turned the cameras off we picked him up laughing to himself and muttering: 'We should just do interviews with him. Just him. He is the only (bleep) I want to speak to ever again. That is genius.' I think he liked the fact it was weird and basically a load of random rubbish.

He was the same as the some of the other actors who moaned about being asked the same old questions. 'We are lucky and in a privileged position,' he said, off camera, this time to me. 'But it's hard being asked the same question 25 times which you can't phrase the same as the one you did before because it's going on a different channel. But then you come up with one that got us talking about Garbage Pail Kids and nicking cola bottles.'

The second time I saw him at his *Total Recall* junket, with the unreal Jessica Biel (lyrics!), he remembered me. The interview went OK but it was what happened afterwards, once the cameras were all off, that I will always remember.

I had heard stories about how back in the day (when he was slurping) he would go into his local pub and shout at the top of his voice: 'For the next hour, all the drinks are on me.' I've wondered if it was like all the great tales about the old Manchester City striker Mario Balotelli that actually turned out to be untrue. Like the one about him driving around Manchester dressed as Santa giving out money. Or the one about him going into a petrol station and paying for all the customers' petrol.

But the best was yet to come. 'I'd love to take you for a night out,' he said. 'You should come out with me one day.'

IS THIS REALLY HAPPENING?

Just imagine... me and wild man Colin Farrell out on the town together? Now that would be carnage I reckon. He was such a top fella and I wish I did go for that night out with him – or several in fact!

CHAPTER 5

SLASHGATE

The interview with Denzel Washington is up there as one of my favourites, no doubt. What a legend that man is.

But the one with Slash, the lead guitarist from Guns N' Roses, is probably the one I get asked about the most, and the one that could have ended my rapping career... or worse! And in a few pages' time you will know exactly why.

When I was younger I loved Guns N' Roses. They were all I listened to, along with MC Hammer and Vanilla Ice of course. The first music I remember buying was MC Hammer's 'U Can't Touch This'. And then it was Guns N' Roses. Lots and lots of their stuff. I bought all their videos on the old VHS too, and then used the cases as pencil cases... come on you know you used to do that too!

One day I nearly got knocked over in their honour. I

was walking down the road to my mum's house with Guns N' Roses blaring out full blast in my Walkman, with a bit of head banging chucked in. 'Welcome To The Jungle' pumping through my headphones was so loud I was totally oblivious to the fact that a car was following me. Later I found out the driver crept up right behind me, but I was so deep in the Guns N' Roses zone I didn't have a clue. I turned off the road to go to my mum's house, leaving one fuming driver behind me. It was only when I got to my mum's house that I found out the car was even there. She had watched me dancing all the way down the road in my own little world and holding up this car behind me.

That was how much I loved Guns N' Roses when I was younger, around 13 or 14. Whether I was in my room, on my bike or on foot, there was a good chance I was listening to them. As much as I could every day.

So imagine the buzz when Helen Chamberlain phoned me up one day and said 'I know someone who is opening up a guitar shop in Epsom called Guitar Guitar. Keep it quiet but Slash is coming to open it and he wants you to go down and do a question for him.' It was obviously not a problem.

'It's Wednesday afternoon, get there at one o'clock, just turn up,' Helen said. 'OK,' I said. 'No worries.' Then, while Helen was still on the phone, all of a sudden the nerves set in. Slash is a legend, especially in my eyes. This was a big interview, both for the show and for me.

So that Wednesday I headed in a car to Epsom with the assistant producer Chris Nutbeam, two cameramen and a sound man. On the way I still hadn't come up with the hard-hitting lyrics I wanted to spit to Slash when I did my rap. I was racking my brains, coming up with ideas that I was dismissing as soon as they came into my head. They just weren't cutting it. At the same time I was also wondering what killer question to ask him.

As it turns out, that particular part of my dilemma turned out to be irrelevant. But more of that later.

Anyhow, as the journey continued and we got closer and closer to Guitar Guitar, I had a lightbulb moment. 'That's it! I've got my rap idea,' I shouted to Chris.

'What?' he said.

'I've got the rap! I've got it. Can we stop up on the way to Epsom?'

'What?' he said, looking totally confused. 'You really are an absolute nutter.'

'You wait until you hear what I've got to say next,' I said to him, buzzing about my brilliant plan. 'I want you to get some ready-made mash potato.'

The look on his face said 'Yeah, do one mate.' But he kept that to himself and a little more politely just said: 'You're a nut.'

Despite that, we stopped off at a convenience shop and walked in. I found some mashed potato but first had an important question to ask. 'Excuse me have you got a microwave?' I said. 'Er, er, yeah, out the back,' the shopkeeper replied. I tried bargaining with them –'I'll pay double for the mash if we can use your microwave as well.'

He had a look on his face that said: 'Why do you want

mashed potato at this time of day?' Bearing in mind it was about 11.30 in the morning. 'It's a long story, don't worry, but is it OK?' I said. 'Can I borrow your micro-wave?' And they agreed! I went through to the back of the shop and heated up my mashed potato, and rather than just leave it in the packaging I stuffed the heated-up mashed potato in my pockets. I thanked the shop-keeper, jumped back into the car and carried on to the guitar shop.

When we arrived the Guitar Guitar shopkeeper was waiting to greet us. 'Thanks so much for coming down, guys,' he says. He didn't need to thank me. I was about to meet Slash – one of my heroes. I should have been thanking him.

The first thing I had to do was explain what I was going to do and why I had mashed potato in my pockets, just so he was in on the plan. He burst out into laughter (the man we needed to be laughing, though, was Slash).

'You want to do that, in a brand-spanking-new shop, that isn't even open yet?' he said. 'It's OK,' I assured him. 'I've got a dust pan and brush and we will clean up any mess we make, so it is fine for when you open, and I've got a Stoke shirt because I heard Slash was a Stoke fan. He can wear that to make sure he doesn't get any on his clothes.'

Meanwhile, this mash potato absolutely stunk and was starting to make me feel sick. Seriously, my eyes were watering and I was gagging every five minutes. And it would not be the last time I felt that way due to food I was using in a stunt I was trying to pull off.

Slash turned up and I began to have serious doubts about what I was planning to do.

Ten minutes after arriving at the shop and gagging numerous times, I was told by one of his disciples (sorry, I mean team): 'Slash is not doing media; he's just doing radio interviews today.'

'What?' I thought. 'What have I been invited down for then?'

'Because we thought it would be funny!' the shop owner said.

'Does Slash know he is doing this?' I asked, getting a little bit worried that I would have to break the news.

'No. I've been a bit cheeky, but it will be good publicity for the shop and we will get your interview,' he promised.

Slash happily did all the radio interviews and it was time for us to get ours. Thankfully the shop owner stepped in and teed him up for us. 'All right, we are just doing one quick TV interview,' he told Slash. 'It's just one question and that is it.' Slash had his glasses on and shrugged 'Oh all right, all right'. He didn't look especially excited about it though.

I offered him the Stoke shirt, because he is from Stoke. 'No,' he said. I had a bad feeling this was going to be awkward. And he hadn't even seen my act yet.

Time wasn't on my side so I hit him with the rap I was prepping in the car on the way over. 'All right Slash, I'm Tubes from *Soccer AM*, I've got One Question and One Question Only. You're a top man you are Slash, some like roasted, but I prefer mash' and dipped into my pockets, filled my hands with the stinking mashed potatoes and smothered it all over my face. 'Oooooh Slash I really love mash.'

He looked at me as if I was out of my mind. He was not happy; he was lucky it was only mash. As soon as it went on my face I honestly thought I was going to be sick. Then, out the corner of my eye, I could see all of his heavies were going ballistic. They were like dogs on leashes waiting for the signal to be let loose so they could tear me to shreds.

Slash broke the silence. 'What kind of response do you think you are going to get. Where did you get that from?'

'The shop,' I said.

'OK, that's a wrap, let's go,' he said, absolutely fuming. 'Yeah, yeah I know,' playing dumb again.

But what he meant was 'that's a wrap', not a rap, as in, that is the end. Finished. I am leaving. And off he stormed.

My response was probably not what anybody in the shop expected. I grabbed my dustpan and brush and started clearing up the mash. So I'm on my knees and these brutes are surrounding me, encouraging me to 'Get the hell outta the shop,' etc., etc., etc.

As I found in even more ridiculous circumstances when I interviewed Bruce Willis, if the celebrity is happy, the heavies are happy. If the celebrity is annoyed, they are annoyed. If the celebrity is cold, they are cold. It's a load of pants really.

Back in Guitar Guitar it was chaos, but I was trying to at least look calm. I had not offended anyone but neither was I prepared to leave the shop with loads of mashed potato on the floor. Duncan Scoble, one of the cameramen, got down as well and was helping me shovel all the mash into the pan. The soundman ran off because he was absolutely bricking it. The other cameraman scarpered too. So it was just me, Duncan Scoble and Chris, left in the shop, all bricking it.

Slash had a serious entourage. There were loads of them. Three of them were towering over me while I was on the floor sweeping up the mash. They were absolutely massive. Proper beasts. They were lucky I didn't bring out the round-the-house sweep though! Ha! Then there were some who didn't move, they just sat at the back of the room having a go at the shop owner for allowing this all to happen. Another three were having a go at Chris.

I am not going to lie. I was scared. They were seriously big and still screaming at me to get out. But I was determined not to leave the shop until it was clean. Mr Muscle would have been proud!

Despite upsetting one of my childhood heroes and being made to fear for my life, there was only one thing that actually upset me that day. After the interview, I walked out of Guitar Guitar. I was covered in mash and had to walk past loads of people, massive Guns N' Roses fans, who were all queuing up to meet Slash, hoping he would do a signing session. This was not to be.

It didn't take long for all those fans who had queued for hours to find out I was the one to blame. It also didn't take long until I started getting abusive hate mail via Twitter and email from some of them.

I tried making it up to them by sending loads of things

out like signed shirts as a way of saying sorry. One particular email stood out though. It was from a mum and dad and said something along the lines of: 'You ruined my son's day. He is only six years old.' I thought: 'How the hell does he know who Guns N' Roses are if he is six years old?' But I wrote them a letter anyway saying I was sorry.

By the following day the story had made the papers. I didn't mind it was in there because it was good publicity for the show and also for the shop. Though the piece did say I attacked Slash with mash and threw it in his face, which obviously was not the case. That made me an even bigger villain in the eyes of his fans. Firstly, for wrecking their chances of getting memorabilia signed, and then for attacking their hero. To this day I still feel bad.

The story also reached the American media. I couldn't believe the reaction. Slash helped repair some of the damage by saying on Twitter 'he didn't throw mash in my face. But he was just some idiot trying to be funny.'

The whole thing went down like a lead balloon. It certainly was not the plan to upset him, or anyone else for that matter. Once I had dealt with all my hate mail, I thought that was the end of that saga, except for a little banter at work. The whole saga got called Slashgate and the week after I had to explain it. At least I was still alive to tell the tale.

It turned out it was far from over, though.

One Sunday morning a week later I was playing football in Croydon for my beloved Oxshott Royals. I had played the day before and got a bit of a knock on my left leg. It got worse as the Sunday game wore on to the point where I had to come off.

By the time I hobbled off and eventually got to my phone I had a few missed calls and text messages from Helen. 'Slash wants your number,' one of the messages said.

I was confused so I called her up. 'Slash's people have phoned up and he wants your number,' she said. 'Oh no,' I thought. 'He wants to give me both barrels now having left it to his heavies last time.'

I went home and it was just a couple of months after my dad passed away. I wasn't in a good way and I did not need this. People already hated me because the joke had gone wrong and now Slash wanted to have his personal say too.

I was with my ex-girlfriend at the time and she could tell something was up. 'What's wrong?' she asked. 'Oh apparently Slash wants my number,' I explained. 'Who's Slash?' she said. 'The guy I... ' 'Oh the guy with the mashed potato?' she twigged.

Meanwhile, my mum was cracking up. 'I have got to hear this conversation,' she said. 'This is going to be classic.'

Later on that day, me and my girlfriend at the time were watching a film at home when my phone rang. It was a private number. This can't be Slash. Surely this is a wind-up.

I didn't answer it.

Half an hour later the phone started ringing again. So I looked at it, private number again, and I didn't answer it. Just left it to ring.

Then we went to a local pub for a drink. We were sitting

in the beer garden and the phone rang again. This time there was a number on the screen that started '00 44... ' At the time I was thinking if this really is a wind-up, it is a good wind-up because whoever is doing it has gone to the lengths of getting a foreign number.

I had had two beers. I was not drunk, but I felt different to when I did at home. This time I picked up the phone.

Tubes: 'Hello?'
Slash: 'Hey Tuuubes.'

This person was clearly American or at least speaking in an American accent.

S: Hey Tuubes it's Slash, Guns N' Roses.
T: Yeah of course it is.
S: No, it's Slash.
T: Yeah nice one mate, now who is it really?
S: Tuubes, it's Slash.
T: Yeah OK, good banter and good impression too. You actually sound like him, but who is it?
S: No, no, no it really is Slash.
T: Is it... ? Really?

If it really was just someone impersonating Slash, they were brilliant. They had had got me. They sounded exactly like him.

SLASHGATE

T: This actually is Slash isn't it?

S: Yeah. It's Slash.'

Then, for some reason he felt he had to apologise.

S: I'm sorry for my behaviour, for my people's behaviour. I heard when I walked off they were all getting in your grill.

T: Yeah, yeah, yeah, but I wasn't trying to upset you.

S: I know, I know. On the way back I checked your stuff out and I like it. I think it is funny. I like it a lot.

I was still confused. Is this still Slash? It was one of my heroes on the other end of the phone, not only apologising but telling me he liked my work.

S: I'm sorry. Next time I'm over we'll meet up. If you are ever in America, if you want to meet up, chill round mine, that's cool.

T: Sorry if I annoyed you.

S: You didn't [bleep] me off. I was just [bleep] off with the people that said no media and then the only media I do that happens with the mash potato. I did say to people no media and there you are chucking mash all over yourself. I wasn't in the mood for it.

To be fair, I couldn't really argue with that.

The whole episode was crazy. Unbelievable. And the ending, Slash inviting me around to his house, just made it even more bizarre.

I was shaking after the phone call. I have still got his number now. Sometimes I wonder whether I should text him and say 'Alright mate?' I have never met him since or been over to the US to see him. We did think about it but haven't done it... it would be quite expensive to fly over just for a couple of minutes of TV.

That day in the guitar shop had been really weird. Slash's entourage were some of the biggest bouncers I have ever seen – all of them well over 6ft 6ins, absolute meatheads, in shorts and covered in tattoos. And there was little me on the floor, with only my little blue dustpan and brush. I wished we had kept the cameras rolling. It would be hilarious to see that now. The one good thing was I got to the end of my cleaning. All the mashed potato was swept up. I am not a rude person and would never chuck mashed potato all over someone's shop and not clean it up.

Despite this episode, I still love Slash all the same. Maybe even more now that he phoned me up and said sorry. He didn't have to do that to someone insignificant as me. He is Slash. Who cares whether I am upset? But it was nice for him to say he looked at some other interviews and he liked them – he even started reeling some of them off. Not that I can remember half of what he said. I was just starstruck. Slash is so big I got starstruck over the phone. It was one of the weirdest phone calls I think I have ever had (the weirdest text was from Chelsea captain John Terry – more on that later).

CHAPTER 6

CHILL OUT, IT'S JUST A LAUGH

So far pretty much all I have given you is the good stuff. How I launched my successful (or not so successful) rapping career, survived a scrape with tough guy Ray Winstone, some Hollywood A-listers I have had a bit of banter with and Jean-Claude Van Damme being 'desperate' to work with me (still think he was pulling my plonker). Even the disastrous Slash/mashed potato interview had a happy ending.

I am starting to sound like one of those doughnuts in the junket waiting room who thinks they're best mates with the big dogs! I can assure you, though, that could not be further from the truth – there are a lot of player haters out there! Inevitably, many interviews have not gone all right on the night and people have been upset along the way, even if it might not have seemed that way by the time you finally saw the footage on *Soccer AM*.

If I had to do a league table of ones that went wrong, my encounter with the actor Steve Coogan, who is most famous for playing Alan Partridge, would win the title by about 20 points. It was easily one of the most awkward interviews I have ever done. It is now even a running joke on the show and in the office how much he hates me, and my god he really does.

I used to love his programme, or most of his programmes when he was playing Alan Partridge – what a genius character by the way – so when I was invited to speak to him I could not wait.

But when I walked into the room I sensed that this might not be as easy as I'd hoped. Not that I let it put me off. I had planned some hard-hitting lyrics – plus, the sole reason he was there was to promote something, so I couldn't see any reason for the idea not to work.

'Hi Steve,' I said, trying to get off on the right foot with a polite welcome.

His response was a totally unenthusiastic 'Hi.'

Instantly I could feel the frostiness. It was colder than the winter months when I was prancing round in a nappy! I tried hitting him with some lyrics to lighten the mood and put a smile on his face. When I finished rapping all he said was 'Yep'.

From this point I knew this was going to be a messy exchange. So I asked him the question. 'Hi Steve. I am Tubes from *Soccer AM*. I've got One Question and One

Question Only. Who is the funniest man in the world in the world, apart from you, ever?'

'Not you!' he said.

In the corner of my eye I spotted a cameraman laughing and making faces and gestures at me as the interview just got more and more awkward by the minute.

> Tubes: Okay.
> Steve Coogan: Not you. It's definitely not you.
> Maybe Ricky Gervais.

I stayed polite to the end and said: 'Thanks very much.' 'Yep.' was all he said back.

It was one of the quickest interviews I have ever done. I went to shake his hand and he gave it a sort of 'You're a dope, get out of this room' kind of slap.

'Thanks a lot mate,' I said.

No response.

'O-kaaay... ' I thought to myself. 'Taxi for Tubes!' That's the only time I have thought 'get me outta here.' At the end when the camera turned off and I thanked him again, all he said was, 'Umm yeah, thanks.'

Steve Coogan just did not find it funny. To this day I don't know why. But am I bovvered?

My interview with Boy George was another bizarre one that went horribly wrong. It was at the Roundhouse in London for some awards do.

The evening didn't start off well when I upset Cheryl Tweedy (as she was then), who was going out with Ashley Cole at the time, during an interview with Girls Aloud. I said to her: 'Hi Cheryl, I'm Tubes from *Soccer AM*. I've got One Question and One Question Only. Who is a better left-back? Ashley Cole or Wayne Bridge?' (knowing full well it would be Ashley Cole).

I thought she would take it the right way as just a bit of banter, but she didn't see the funny side at all and just shot back at me, 'Ashley Cole.' She wasn't happy but the other four girls were cracking up, which probably didn't help.

So I moved on to Boy George (sounds weird). At the time there were loads of people outside banging on the windows and shouting loads of stuff at him while I interviewed him in this enclosed room.

I asked him something about football... and his reaction was totally unexpected. 'I don't even like football,' he shot back at me. 'Why are you asking me about football, I don't even like football? Do you think I care?' Then he starts sparring verbally with all the people outside the room.

What he wasn't to know at the time was that ITN were there too. And they caught the entire incident on camera, which made great footage for their news bulletins the next day.

Tim thought it was classic and we showed it on the show because in the background you can see me looking horrified. It was quite early into the days of me being let off the leash and out into the big wide world to interview people, so I really was wondering what the hell I had done.

But while I was panicking, Tim was just cracking up and saying: 'Now the Tubes beast has been created. Look at the reactions you're getting. We have created a monster here. You've already made the ITN News.'

Thankfully the news report left me out of it and didn't point the finger at me, just concentrating on Boy George. But I confess that it was actually me who sparked the whole thing off with a question he didn't want to answer.

I had met Boy George at a red-carpet event, which is what I started out doing before going to all the film junkets. My brief chat with Ian Brown from The Stone Roses at another red-carpet event was equally a shocker.

I met him at the premiere of Manchester United god Ryan Giggs's DVD *True Red*. The night had started so well, with Cristiano Ronaldo replying with one of the funniest answers to One Question and One Question Only. Manchester United defender Rio Ferdinand rolled up with Anderson and his then teammate Cristiano Ronaldo and they were all blanking all the sports news and news channels. Luckily Rio Ferdinand spotted me waiting for interviews so they came over. 'Yes Tubes, yes Tubes,' Rio said, as he dragged the other two over. Cristiano Ronaldo didn't fancy it and I could see him saying 'no, no, no, no, no,' while Anderson couldn't really speak English and also didn't look keen.

I did a rubbish rap to them and asked: 'Who is the best player in the world ever?'

Rio Ferdinand didn't hesitate with his answer. 'Maradona,' he fired back straight away. I am not sure Anderson totally understood the question and copied Rio Ferdinand because he mumbled: 'M-m-m-m-m-m-Maradona,' and the other guys just started laughing at him. Then it was Cristiano Ronaldo's turn and his answer was surprising, in some ways, but also hilarious, because it was so unexpected. 'Me,' he said. And off he walked. To be fair to him, he has to be up there, doesn't he?

Ian Brown was one of the next famous names I collared that night. I delivered a little rap to him. 'Hi Ian, I'm Tubes from *Soccer AM*. I have got One Question and One Question Only. You're a top man, you're Ian Brown, here it is my bad boy frown,' I said, before pulling one of many silly faces.

Like Cristiano Ronaldo, he didn't hang around either. 'You've got to keep off the droogs, mate,' he said in his strong Mancunian accent and he was off.

Hollywood star Samuel L. Jackson was another who didn't take too well to me. I was interviewing him and the fit actress Scarlett Johansson at the same time at a junket (they were in the film *The Spirit* together).

After baffling them with a rap that made both of them think there was something wrong with me (I promise you there isn't) and putting Scarlett Johansson on edge by telling her that she is fit multiple times, I asked them what film they would work in together that has already been made. Seeing them sat next to each other, this bright spark decided to suggest *Beauty and the Beast*.

The smirk on Samuel L. Jackson's face quickly changed to a look that basically said 'I'm going to knock you out'. He was not happy. Not happy at all. 'I don't like that. I don't like that idea at all,' he said menacingly. Meanwhile, Scarlett Johansson was cracking up.

They may be some of the interviews that have ended badly, but at least I got them. Which is more than what I can say for another actor – Daniel Craig. I have never interviewed the latest James Bond and I don't really fancy my chances of ever getting him because he point-blank refuses to speak to *Soccer AM*.

Bizarrely, I actually found out he was anti-Tubes after being invited to meet him. We were approached by the people who plug the film and asked if we wanted to interview him before his first film as the new James Bond.

For us it was an instant yes and I was buzzing about meeting James Bond and asking him One Question and One Question Only, which was going to be 'What is the best James Bond film ever made?'

But then they shot us down with their reply. 'Actually Daniel Craig doesn't want to do this interview,' we were told. Now every time something comes up and we make the request we get the same answer. 'No. Daniel Craig does not want to do this interview.' They have said it is because he's watched some of the interviews I've done and doesn't like what he's seen.

The more rejections I get from Daniel Craig, the more determined I am to get him, though. You can't shake me off that easily.

The actor Simon Pegg gives me hope that one day I can change Daniel Craig's opinion and persuade him to sit down for a *Soccer AM* interview. If only he will give me the chance. Simon Pegg also didn't like me first time round when I met him at a red-carpet event, ironically for a new James Bond film. Nick Frost, another actor who has worked with Simon Pegg in loads of TV shows and films, was also there.

Nick loves *Soccer AM* so he was straight over, all 'Hey, how you doing Tubes?' and he happily answered a question on the red carpet. He kept saying how much he loved *Soccer AM* and invited me in to the premiere. He even said I could sit next to him, which was a very kind offer.

Then he brought Simon Pegg over, who I thought would be OK, purely because he was Nick Frost's mate. I did a rap to Simon Pegg and his response was a less than flattering 'That's rubbish.' Then he said 'I don't even like football and I'm not interested.' Charming! From that point on he refused to do junkets with me and I always had to speak to Nick on his own.

Then, when I went along to the junket before their film *Paul*, I was told I was speaking to Simon Pegg and Nick Frost together. Given our rocky relationship, surely somebody, somewhere had made a mistake, I thought. 'Are you sure?' I asked the organisers, 'because Simon Pegg refuses to speak to me.' But, no, Simon Pegg did the interview with Nick Frost and he was brilliant, a real nice bloke (who I can't remember making a slightly bad film). Afterwards he was even tweeting me calling me a 'hero of England, top man Tubes'. He was telling all his followers about this great interview and how I was a scholar of the people. What a turnaround.

I have no idea what happened. Maybe it was my improved lyrical flow: 'Hi guys I'm Tubes from *Soccer AM*. I've got One Question and One Question Only. You're top guys you're a comedy pair, when I get angry, rooooooaaaaarrrrr, I'm like a grizzly bear... grizzly, grizzly bear.'

I kept my cool as we had a laugh, but inside I was thinking: 'How the hell has this happened? For four or five years he didn't even want to speak to me.' Part of me wanted to ask him why he didn't want to speak to me previously, but I decided not to – it wasn't worth dragging it all up.

I was genuinely nervous about that interview because I thought he didn't like me. But he really is all right. Maybe he followed my career for a bit and thought 'That Tubes guy is all right really'? Actually, thinking about it, he probably didn't.

TUBES EXTRA

TOP TEN RAPS

To Peter Shilton: 'You're a top man, you are Shilts, I'm flying high, it's like I'm on stilts.'

To Monty Panesar: 'Monty Monty Panesar, I bet you've got a right nice car, Ferrari, Mercedes-Benz, Ooooo you can spin ball from both ends.'

To Denzel Washington: 'You're a top man you're Big Den, I have been rapping since I was 10, Ooooo rapping's for life, not just for Christmas.'

To David Ginola: 'You're top man, you're Ginola, I've got a fetish Ooooo cherry cola.' (Pour can of cherry cola over my head.)

TUBESOLOGY

To The Rock: 'I'm in love with Trevor Brooking, can you smell lalalalalalala what the Tubes is cooking? It doesn't matter what the Tubes is cooking!' (Followed by 'the people's eyebrow'.)

To Russell Brand: 'You're proper bare, you've got cool hair, you know how to pull a chick, oh my gosh these lyrics are sick Ooooo you can't stop the bad man.'

Alesha Dixon: 'When I say Savile, you say Row, Savile (audience: Row), Savile (Row), Savile (Row), look at me now you can't say no.'

Professor Green: 'You're sitting there, all lyrical waxy [get phone out of my pocket], yeah OK mate, you might as well go, because I've booked you a taxi.'

Ryan Jarman: 'The cribs – you're top man, you're a crib, when I was a baby I wore a bib Ooooo dribble dribble... Sybil [*Fawlty Towers*] style.'

Craig David: 'You're standing there, you're Craig David, sorry bruv these lyrics are sacred, shhhshhh I can't tell you any more.'

CHAPTER 7

I LOVE GIRLS, GIRLS, GIRLS, GIRLS I DO ADORE...

A s my good friend Jay Z once said: 'I love girls, girls, girls, girls, girls I do adore.' If there is one type of interview I want to nail every single time, it is the one with the lovely ladies.

Thanks to *Soccer AM* I have had the chance to try and impress and strip in front of some of the fittest women in the world. For a few minutes there is a little part of me that thinks that I have got a chance to go out with one of them. (Alesha I haven't given up). All I have to do is just play my cards right.

In my desperation to impress, though, what tends to happen is that I bottle it big time and end up spouting nonsense instead of sick lyrics!

That is exactly what happened the day we had the amazing actress Nadine Velazquez from *My Name is Earl* on the show. I have never screwed my lines up as badly as I did on this fateful day. And the worst thing was pretty much everyone knew it was coming. Even me, despite my best attempts to hide it.

As soon as I found out she was on there was no way I was going to pass up the opportunity to speak to her. But I had worked myself up to the point that I was struggling to get any words out from the moment I stepped onto the set.

Helen and Max both knew me well and knew that I was going to be distracted by Nadine Velazquez sitting on the sofa. Helen started introducing the interview I had done during the week with Liam Neeson, but to be honest I wasn't paying the slightest bit of attention. Instead I was just staring at Nadine Velazquez on the sofa.

Helen: All right Tubes?

Tubes: How you doing?

H: Good. You met Liam Neeson in the week then, Tubes?

T: Yep.

H: I hope so because we have been trailing it all the show.

T: Yeah I did.

H: Was he nice?

T: Yeah he was really nice.

By this point I was already gone. Talking to Helen but thinking about Nadine Velazquez and grabbing a cheeky look whenever I could.

> H: What you looking at?
> T: All right.

I nodded at Nadine Velazquez, trying to be a bit of a cheeky chappy but also a bit cool. The whole studio started cracking up, even some of the guests next to her on the sofa. It was already pretty clear that I was basically in love.

We cut to the Liam Neeson video for a couple of minutes, which bought me some time to gather my thoughts, try and regain some of my composure and also keep staring at Nadine Velazquez before it was time to ask her the question.

> Helen: Tubes, you've got One Question and One
> Question Only, who is your question to?
> Tubes: It's for Nadine.
> H: Oh yeah? Ohhh scary...
> T: You're in *My Name is Earl*, you're pretty swell,
> oh my gosh, I love you, oh I don't know what
> I've just done... '

Cue more raucous laughter from everyone in the studio at my expense, again led by Helen and the crew, as I ballsed up my rap like never before.

> Helen: Oh Tubes.
> Max: Again, again, again. It is totally
> understandable how that could happen.
> H: I must say I could see that coming. Is it the
> pretty lady that has put you off, Tubes?

T: Yes.

H: Ahhhhh, Tuuuubes, would you like another go?

T: No thanks.

I couldn't do it again. At this point my head was gone and the situation was beyond saving. My face was a picture too, having put myself through the horror of watching it back. I wanted to laugh too but was also beyond embarrassed. I was just left standing there like a bit of an idiot with an awkward-looking smirk on my face.

H: But have you got a question still?

T: Yeah.

H: Okay, go on then.

While everyone was still laughing at me rather than with me, I had to try and compose myself.

Tubes: When are we going for a drink?

Nadine Velazquez: Tonight.

T: Tonight?

N: Tonight.

T: Oh what a touch.

And with that I was out. Job done.

When you bomb your mind just goes blank and you just want the ground to open up and swallow you. Unfortunately I am speaking from experience! Even though I stayed to ask the question I couldn't wait to get off. I have never walked off set so quickly in my life (apart from after the first shambolic question to Frank Worthington).

I was like a defender, who has just been sent off for a horrific two-footed tackle or a last-man foul. You know it is a red card. Just walk.

I can't even remember what I was going to say to her. Even to this day. But even from what I did manage to get out you could tell by the look on her face that she was wondering what the hell it was all about! Hopefully I rescued that car crash moment by at least getting her to say yes to a date, which of course never happened – I stopped returning her calls!

The outrageously fit Carmen Electra and Eva Mendes also said yes when I asked them for dates too. I know they only say it to humour me, and when Carmen Electra said yes I just clammed up all of a sudden. I was expecting her to shoot me down on TV but she said: 'Oh all right, we'll do Wednesday.'

Just in case you are wondering, we didn't meet up and no, she hasn't been in touch either

Jessica Biel was another stunner who kindly didn't shoot me down. Well, not to my face anyway. This interview could have gone horribly wrong as I didn't do my research before I met her and know that her and Justin Timberlake – her now husband, lucky FFFFF... fella – had split up at the time I actually got asked before the interview by one of her 'people': 'You are not going to ask about Justin Timberlake, are you?'

'Why would I talk about that?' I asked.

'Well they've just split up.'

'Oh!' was all I could manage, a little embarrassed that I didn't know. But I wriggled my way out of it and explained we were not there to stitch anyone up, we just wanted to have a bit of a laugh.

That is exactly what we did because she got the humour of the interview straight away. The One Question and One Question Only I asked her was: 'If you could go to one place in the world you haven't been to yet, where would you go?' Straight away Jessica Biel said: 'Egypt. Your house in Egypt.'

The interview went so well and we were talking (well, she was talking and I was staring at her) for so long that I had to cut it down for the show because it ran on for so long. She was giving me advice about how to be more attractive to the ladies like shave my chest hair off and she loved doing a stare off with me. I reckon it must have been my eyes!

One of the organisers of the junket even phoned me afterwards and told me Jessica Biel had said she'd really enjoyed the interview and that it was so much fun.' I sent her a message on Twitter a couple of days later saying: 'I have bought my house in Egypt. It is ready for you to come over.' She replied 'Haha. Good interview.' In other words: 'Nooooo, do one you freak!' But she is back with Justin Timberlake now, so it's safe to say I missed out there.

Jessica Biel has got the best body I have ever seen. I remember her walking past me in the corridor and all I could think was: 'Wow, wow, wow.'

I must admit it is a bit weird basically just staring at an unbelievably attractive woman and drooling, especially as I am not like that at all. Actually it is more than a bit weird,

Above left: How it all began: Peter the Test Tube Baby in action, complete with can of beer and fake cigarette. *(All imagery courtesy of BSkyB Ltd.)*

Above right: Film hardman Ray Winstone: 'I was getting ready to do a runner… '

Below: The legend that is Denzel Washington – one of my funniest interviews ever.

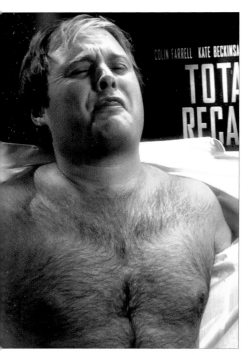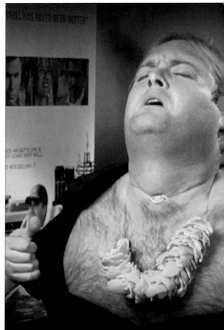

The Tubes rapping style (clockwise from top left): to Jessica Biel; in my orange-peel necklace for Will Ferrell; to Jim Carrey; and a double-rap with my younger brother, Big Ange.

It doesn't always go to plan… (top to bottom): rubbing mashed potato into my face for Slash ended in what I call 'Slashgate'; and I managed to upset Cheryl Cole (then Cheryl Tweedy) when I interviewed her and her band, Girls Aloud; while Boy George said 'Why are you asking me about football, I don't even like football?' – sparking an incident that ended up on the national news.

There are compensations (clockwise from top left): the 'outrageously fit' Carmen
Electra; Jessica Alba, who declined to give me tips to pull a fit girl like her; Nicole
Scherzinger – she was lovely, and 'her troll impression was probably one of the
funniest things I've seen a celebrity do'; and in a Savile Row suit to interview
Alesha 'she is so fit' Dixon (sigh…).

Above left: Will Ferrell – 'a solid, genuine guy unaffected by Hollywood glitz'.

Above right: Jim Carrey – I taught him the Chelsea 'Celery' chant in another hilarious interview.

Below: Sylvester Stallone – he admitted that Arnie is harder.

Above left: Professor Green – a top bloke, and my rap battle with him remains an epic event.

Above right: Another absolute legend, Hulk Hogan. His choke hold on me was not in the script, but he was as nice as could be.

Below: 50 Cent – another top rapper who got into the spirit of things.

Above: Wladimir Klitschko – I was astonished by how clever the boxer is, and a top bloke, as well.

Middle: Joe Hart, the Manchester City and England goalkeeper, 'one of the nicest people I've met in football'.

Below: Theo Walcott – the Arsenal and England player was once an 'underwear bandit' with his friend Gareth Bale.

Above left: Graeme Souness – despite being as tough as nails, 'he was a really good laugh and really interesting'.

Above right: Kevin Keegan – 'another "did that really happen?" moment, Kevin Keegan and me, spraying each other with perfume'.

Below: 'Chelsea are my team and blue is the colour' – me with Ashley Cole and John Terry. What could be better?

it is really weird, because it just not the done thing. Neither is ripping my top open and getting my moobs out though, I must admit.

But it is all part of an act and just for TV. I promise!

Fortunately all the lovely ladies mentioned in this chapter have taken it the right way and been nice to me. Well, all except the actress Jessica Alba, that is, when I met her at her junket for *The Eye*.

Firstly, some praise. She is also so fit in real life. I had walked into the room and instantly gone, 'Wow, she is proper fit,' and I thought she was going to be a good laugh. And it looked that way after my rap, which got what seemed like a genuine laugh...

Tubes: Hi Jessica I am Tubes from *Soccer AM*, I have got One Question and One Question Only. You're so hot, you're so pretty, let's get down to the nitty-gritty, ooooohhhhhh you're so fit.'

Jessica Alba: Okay. That was good. What was the question?

I started acting up, giving her that weird stare of mine and drooling.

T: I think I am in love.

JA: Oh really. I think you are delusional.

But I carried on properly staring at her and doing the drooling act. She did not have a clue what was going on and started getting a bit uncomfortable. We were only a few minutes in but already I could see her looking at her entourage, who were in the room but off camera, for help. I could also hear them whispering, asking whether it was already time to pull the interview because I was seriously playing up.

I think they thought I was some crazed fan who had somehow managed to blag their way into the junket and get up close and personal with Jessica Alba. I thought it was going to be a situation where her 'people' swarmed in all of a sudden and started screaming at me: 'What are you doing? What are you doing?' A bit like Slash's heavies. But they let it go and let me carry on my act. For a little while, anyway.

The One Question and One Question Only was: 'You are really fit and really good-looking. But I really want to pull a fit girl like you so have you got any tips please?' She gave me a lame answer but I tried to convince her that I fitted the bill for her and that me and her should get together.

JA: Errr, no.
T: Oh

She just kept laughing at me, rubbing in the rejection and had no idea I was mucking around while still giving her my special, weird, slightly deranged stare.

JA: Yeah, no. I am taken.
T: Lucky fella.
JA: He is pretty lucky I might say. I am pretty lucky too.

T: Okay, thank you.

JA: Thank you.

When I finished I thought: 'Well, this is awkward, I've got to get out of here quickly.'

And as I packed up I could hear her asking her entourage: 'What the hell was that? That guy is seriously weird. That is the strangest man I have ever met. That is one strange man.'

I just grabbed my stuff and walked out of there. Quickly. I think she thought I was being serious and was actually trying to pull her. I don't think I will be seeing her again. In fact I'm pretty certain of that.

After the interview some of the others were trying to explain to her that my slightly dopey personality is all part of the joke. Well, her entourage were not laughing. 'That is a bit weird mate,' one of them said to me. I tried to reason with them and tell them I am not being serious. 'Well, what is the point of that?' they said. 'It's a bit of a laugh,' I replied. 'Okay, well that's not really for us.' 'All right then,' I said, and toddled off.

When these situations get awkward I must admit I don't really care. Whatever the reaction is it makes all-right TV (I hope).

You turn up at these events and are told 'you can't say this to them and you can't say that to them' – that is probably why some of them are like the way they are, a bit stiff and occasionally stroppy.

When someone like Leonardo Di Caprio or Denzel Washington says 'That was awesome' as you are leaving and asks you to come back again, that proves most of them like being interviewed about slightly different things.

But the entourages that some of them have do make things unnecessary. Once I turned up to a Bruce Willis junket for one of his *Die Hard* films and received one of the weirdest instructions I have ever had from one of his people. 'You can't do the rap with Bruce there,' they said. 'What do you mean?' I asked, totally baffled. 'Just do it to an empty chair and he can then come in and do the interview.' 'I'm not doing that. I'd rather go home,' I said. 'We'll leave you to the end then,' they said back.

A few hours later, while I was still waiting for my interview, four men came hurtling out of the room where he was holding his interviews and hurried off down the corridor of the Dorchester Hotel.

'Wow that looks serious,' I said to one of the women organising the junket. 'What's happened? Has he passed out or something? Is he all right?' 'Nah, he's hungry,' she said.

Personally, I thought it was a bit strange to be charging around to get some food as if it was an emergency, but then I'm not a Hollywood star. Unbelievable Jeff!

CHAPTER 8

OOOOO
FRUITY

Will Ferrell is a solid genuine guy unaffected by Hollywood glitz. He has won more awards than I have had hot dinners, and trust me I have had a lot of them. Yet he could not be more down to earth if he tried. He is one of the coolest and funniest men I have ever met.

I have now had the privilege of speaking to him a few times. The first was so long ago I can't even remember what it was for, but I remember him saying he liked the interview because it was 'out there, dude'. He was just like how he appears in his films. He was a Chelsea fan too, which always gets you extra points in my book.

He enjoyed the first interview so much he asked if I could go to his next junket and now I do all of them when he is in England.

The second time I met him I wanted to come up with

something a bit special. I didn't want to put him through the same routine but instead freshen it up and try and catch him off guard with something he was not expecting. Obviously it helped that I knew he enjoyed all the messing about and would take it the right way.

Before meeting Will Ferrell again at his junket for *Everything Must Go*, I spent a lot of my time thinking what I could do. None of the ideas were grabbing me. I just wasn't in the lyrical zone, and for this one I needed to be.

I still hadn't nailed it down when I was in the car on the way over to the hotel I had got the start: 'You're a great guy, you are Will… ' But it was the ending that was proving a problem. 'I like fish and chips like Ian Beale… ', 'Kill Bill', 'window seal' were all phrases that came into my head as potential lyrics. I was trying to come up with words that rhyme with his name but nothing was really jumping out and grabbing me.

The car was getting closer and I still didn't have my rap. The clock was ticking. Then, for some reason 'orange peel' came into my head. Yes, orange peel.

Just before the car arrived, I turned to my good mate and colleague 'Lavvers', who at the time was also the props guy.

Totally straight-faced I said: 'Can you make me an orange peel necklace?' He said: 'What are you on? You're mental, aren't you?' It was like the reaction when I'd asked for mash on my way to meet Slash, all over again. Lavvers did it anyway and, to be fair to him, he absolutely nailed it. He found some fishing wire, loads of orange peel to make the necklace and I put it around my neck, and underneath my shirt. Then we jumped in the car, all strapped up and ready to go.

On my way to the hotel for the junket I stunk of orange. Absolutely stunk. And obviously my shirt was poking out too, even more so than it does with my truffle-shuffle belly.

When we arrived at the hotel I had to walk past plenty of people to get to the waiting room. Pretty much every person started sniffing the air curiously after I breezed by. 'What are you wearing?' loads of people asked me. I just lied. 'It's just a new aftershave.' 'You smell like a fruit,' was a common answer. Little did they know there was a very good reason for that...

I tried fobbing them off but it must have been so obvious I had something underneath my shirt and many of them just wouldn't let it go. 'It smells like an orange or a lemon, some kind of fruit.' I'm just nodding along 'Yeah, yeah, it's just a new aftershave – Orange by Jordan, innit.' In my head, though, I was thinking: 'You properly stink of orange. Stink.'

I did my usual thing of slumping into the corner, keeping myself to myself by playing snake. And this time I really did want to be ignored.

When I got the call to say it was my turn to speak to Will Ferrell I was out of the door like a shot. I walked in and straight away members of his entourage clocked there was something sticking out underneath my shirt. They were probably on alert, thinking I had a gun or something under there.

Will Ferrell saved me from getting completely taken out before I had even sat down though by screaming: 'Heeeyyyy, hey Tuuubes, how's it going? I'm ready for the next instalment of Tuubes.' The edgy entourage all relaxed, realised I was all right, and stood down again. Once again, the celebrity was all right, so they were all right.

It was time for the big reveal, so I launched into my rap. 'Hi Will, I'm Tubes from *Soccer AM*, I've got One Question and One Question Only. You're a top man, you are Will, I have got a fetish, oooooh orange peel, oh Will I really love orange peel,' and ripped open my shirt to reveal the necklace.

He was stunned. 'You're mental,' he laughed, 'what are you doing?' Then we started talking about citrus fruits and which ones were our favourites for a few minutes.

'I like lemons,' he said. 'What about kumquats? Actually, they are not really a citrus fruit.' It was that kind of nonsense.

He was obviously intrigued by the necklace creation and asked how long it took me to make. 'I've had it on since I was 14,' I said, with a completely straight face.

Even though it was a bit strange what I was doing, Will Ferrell was laughing, so his heavies were too.

Now if he was to look at me and say 'What are you doing?' they will look at me exactly the same as him. But when I walked out they were giving me high fives and Will even gave me a cuddle.

The first time around is always weird because people don't know what's going on, especially the Americans. I don't know if they don't find it funny or if they think: 'Are you trying to take the mickey out of these people?'

But that is one thing I never try and do. I'm not like Dennis Pennis who asks rude questions. I just like to see the other side of the personality not the same old, same old 'yeah the film is really good' stuff, and that is why most of the celebs enjoy it. You know, talking about orange peel is different. I doubt that came up in any of Will Ferrell's other interviews.

The Americans can be a bit funny and precious – the Bruce Willis rapping to the empty chair was a classic example. But Will Ferrell was brilliant. The third time he greeted me with, 'Heeeyyy Tuuubes, how's your orange peel fetish?' so he obviously remembered, and I had to explain I had been in rehab to get over the addiction since the last time I saw him, but was on the road to recovery.

Because he was in such a good mood I pushed my luck and asked him to do a wedding message for me, as I was soon to be best man at one of my best mates' weddings. Gary (who's the spitting image of Screech from *Saved By the Bell*) and his now wife are huge fans of Will Ferrell. They love him..

But it meant I had to break a career-long rule to ask for something personal from one of the celebs. I never do it. Never ask for photos, autographs, anything. But this time I had to. I was best man, and panicking about my speech. I had to ask Will Ferrell because any contribution from him or Seth Rogen would be the icing on the wedding cake.

As this was the third time I had met Will Ferrell I thought I had at least a chance so at the end of the interview I plucked up the courage to ask. 'Look Will, I'm really sorry but basically my mate is getting married,' and his people straight away jumped in with 'No, no, no, no, no.'

But he shot them down instantly. 'Yes, yes, yes, yes,' he

said. It was funny to see the entourage silenced again. They sat back down. Meanwhile he got more and more interested and excited about doing a bit for the wedding speech. 'Will I be on a big screen and stuff?' he asked.

It was weird seeing Will Ferrell get excited about being on a big screen in front of just 100 or so people when his films are watched by millions. 'Yeah, yeah, OK I'll do it. What are their names?' he asked. 'Gary and Gemma,' I told him

He just sat in his chair for about 30 seconds, thinking. He was deep, deep in thought. Then he snapped out of it and shouted 'Roll' and started delivering his message into the camera.

He went on for about two and a half minutes, canning Gemma, canning Gary, even though he didn't know the anything about them. 'Don't worry about it. It will be fine,' he reassured me when he finished.

By the time the wedding came around and I was doing the speech I thought I'd actually done quite well, telling all the stories I'd prepared myself. But the best was yet to come. The centrepiece.

'Finally,' I began, 'some people obviously couldn't make it to the wedding today, Gary and Gemma, so they've left you a message.'

There was one from Seth Rogen. It was a simple: 'Sorry I can't be there today but I've got better things to do. Sorry.' Everyone reacted OK. There was a sprinkling of laughter in the room and I heard a few say 'That is quite funny.'

Then Will Ferrell's face came on the projector screen and the whole room was in tears, straight away. He was saying things like: 'We are a trio now, all part of one big relationship,' and 'I will be on our honeymoon next week,' and 'I've heard you got a really loud mouth and you're always talking Gemma!' (which she does – only joking Gems!)

In a way his speech was too good and I got worried she would think that I had told Will Ferrell all that stuff. So I had to prep Gemma before the wedding to warn her about the video but not to tell Gary. He was totally in the dark. Thankfully she loved it. 'That's awesome, that's awesome,' she kept repeating over and over again. It was a huge relief because I didn't want her to start crying or anything like that on her big day.

Afterwards, Will Ferrell said: 'Was that cool? Was that all right, Tubes?'

But it was better than that. It was amazing. And all the guests wanted DVD copies of the speech. I had to get 20 or 30 made after the wedding, so luckily Sky helped me out with that.

The whole speech went down well and everyone was saying it was the best best-man speech they had ever heard. But it was only because Will Ferrell helped me out massively. It was nothing to do with me.

TUBES EXTRA

TOP TEN INTERVIEW QUOTES

'That's my claim to fame mate, I got Tubes all flustered'

— Tim Cahill

'Quit tickling the palm of my hand with your finger'

— Hulk Hogan

'You're crazy man'

— 50 Cent

'We should do interviews with just him, just him, he is the only f****r I ever want to speak to again when selling a film'

— Colin Farrell

'I think you're delusional'

— Jessica Alba

TUBESOLOGY

'Kill yourself'   – Jim Carrey

'You've got to keep off the drugs, mate'   – Ian Brown

'Your country needs you'   – Hugh Jackman

'The traffic down here, a 5-minute journey can take you
15 to 20 minutes. Up in Sheffield, you can get somewhere
that's supposed to take you five minutes in four minutes'
                                                       – a Kyle Walker

'It looks like you want to hit me'   – Bradley Cooper

'You're so fit'   – Jessica Biel

'Cheers for the interview brother, right on bro. Good
straight face too, you keep it going... that was awesome'
                                                       – Leonardo DiCaprio

'Why are you asking me this? I hate football' – Boy George

CHAPTER 9

NI– TROLL SCHERZINGER

As you have probably guessed, I love it when I can get a celebrity to let their guard down. It is so refreshing to see them in a totally different light.

I try to treat them like human beings as much as possible, rather than the untouchable heroes that their entourages think they are All human beings like to laugh, so I don't see why celebrities wouldn't like a laugh and bit of banter. That is my general attitude anyway.

Because of that, I think that is why I don't mind asking them to do bizarre things when other people might think, 'you can't get so and so to do that'. Why not, is my view?

Nicole Scherzinger's troll impression was probably one of the funniest things I have ever seen a celebrity do. I met the former Pussycat Dolls singer and ridiculously fit *X-Factor* judge at Westfield Shopping Centre in Shepherd's Bush

She was doing a launch for one of her sponsors where she had to do a demonstration in a room backstage that was being projected onto a big screen outside which all the audience could see. Then she had to come out and show off a pair of trainers. It did not seem like the most taxing thing I have ever seen.

But it was cold and wet and she did not sound keen. 'It's too cold'... 'I'm not going to start jogging'... 'Ooooohhhhh it's freezing and they want me to run around out there' – that sort of stuff.

I was supposed to be speaking to her after her little bit of modelling and was thinking: 'This is going to be awful. The last thing she wants is some odd guy drooling over her and making stupid faces when she is feeling the cold. At least I get to see Nicole Scherzinger in real life though, I thought... even though I was scared that my interview slot might get scrapped altogether because she was not happy. There were thousands of people there to see her – why would she care about me?

But when she walked off stage and came into the room for the interview she was lovely. Totally professional. She was wearing a really tight-fitting outfit which, I must admit, influenced my view of her, too.

Once I put her at ease that she wasn't going to have to talk about football, I cheered her up with a little freestyle:

> Tubes: Hi Nicole, I'm Tubes from *Soccer AM*, I've got One Question and One Question Only.
> Nicole Scherzinger: Okay.
> T: You're a top girl, you're Nicole, here's my

impression of a troll [I launched into a quick
routine of a funny face and few funny noises]...
oooooohhhhh, let's get married.

Given how she was before this could have sent her over
the edge and stomping back to her dressing room in
disgust. But my lyrics actually put a smile on her face and
got her laughing.

NS: Errrrr, that is yeah... if I was a judge on *X-
Factor* I'm not sure how I would feel about that.
But, erm. I liked... erm... the ambition behind it.
T: You're so fit.
NS: And. Errrr. You're fit as well. And I liked the
troll impression.
T: Thank you. You're a great girl. And I love you.
What I want to know is, what would be your
perfect day?
NS: Hanging out with you.
T: Really? Let's do it.
NS: That would be my perfect day.
T: Where would we go?
NS: We would go troll hunting.

It seemed too good to be true and she must have suspected
what was coming next.

T: Go on then. What is your impression of a
troll?

And she just launched into one, with hardly any encouragement needed at all. Her troll impression was brilliant too. It was complete with actions and great sound effects. It has to be seen to be believed. Someone like Nicole Scherzinger doing a troll impression. Hilarious. You could tell she absolutely loved mucking around and doing it, too.

And I left thinking 'What a nice girl.' Stunning too. Beautiful and brilliant. Before I really thought the whole thing was going to get called off, but I ended up leaving with one of the funniest bits of footage I have ever got.

I surprise myself sometimes with the answers and requests I come up with when I'm put on the spot. When I walk away from the interview I often think: 'How on earth have you come up with that?'

It was like the Denzel Washington one when he said: 'What would your mum and dad think about what you are doing right now?' And it just came to me straight away: 'They would be like "Wow, you are meeting Big Denzel."' I have no idea where that idea came from! After it came out of my mouth I thought 'Did I really just say that?'

I suppose when you are under pressure and you're trying to entertain your mind goes into freak mode. It's difficult to explain.

Sometimes people come with me to interviews because they want to meet a certain celebrity. On this occasion my mate Bobby Chalal, who works at *Soccer AM*, came along because he absolutely loves Nicole Scherzinger. And he said: 'How do you do that? Come up with the rap and all the ideas?' And I couldn't answer him. It's all just in my rather strange head.

It's weird watching the interviews later because it doesn't seem like me. It was funny walking away from that one thinking that I got Nicole Scherzinger to do a troll impression. When I told people, they just didn't believe me. Then they saw it and just kept asking 'How have you done that?'

When people say that I think why wouldn't they? Just because they're in films or on TV? If you like having a laugh, you have a laugh. I guess the fact it happens so rarely is what makes it weird to see a celebrity do things like that. Fair play to the ones who do.

Believe it or not though, Nicole Scherzinger's troll impression is far from the weirdest thing I have managed to persuade a celebrity to do. That award would probably go to Gerard Butler, who I convinced to try and chat me up in another random interview.

Now Gerard Butler is a class actor and been in plenty of films, some of them really big. The biggest was probably *300*. He won loads of awards for playing Spartan King Leonidas in that. But it was pretty clear he had never been asked to do what I made him do when I rocked up to his junket for his film *Playing for Keeps*. He knew the show and is a Celtic fan so we started off with a bit of banter before I impressed him with a *300*-related rap that he seemed to like:

'Hi Gerard, I'm Tubes from *Soccer AM*. I've got One Question and One Question Only. You're a top man, you're Gerard, it's not my fault that I'm this hard [rips shirt open... again] ooooohhhhh, I. Am. Sparta, rooooooaaaaarrrrrr, these lyrics are really, really sick.'

Then it was on to the question. Gerard Butler is known as a bit of a ladies' man and his girlfriend at the time was the stunning, model Madalina Ghenea, so that provided the inspiration I needed.

'You're a top bloke and I love you. You're a great actor. You love your football and also the ladies fancy you. You pull some fit girls. I'm struggling with the ladies, so can you show me, how to pull a lady?'

I could see him squirm a little bit, straight away. But I didn't even give him a chance to say no or wriggle out of this one and immediately started setting the scene. 'I'm in a nightclub, I'm a good-looking girl and I start dancing, and you have to pull me,' I said.

You could tell from his face he wasn't overly keen on this and was wondering what it was all about.

I started dancing anyway. Sensing there was no way out, he just got involved:

Tubes: How are you doing? You all right?'
Gerard Butler: I'm good. Listen, I have got to say, you're not normally my type. Normally I don't go for girls with as big boobs as you, but you'll do.
T: Thank you. You?
GB: Can I buy you a drink?
T: Yes please.
GB: Do you want to just take the money for the drink and call it a day?
T: No you're all right. I'll have a drink.
GB: (bleep).

He was hoping I'd say no so he didn't have to carry this whole awkward act on.

> GB: Okay. I guess you better follow me. All the way to my hotel room.
> T: Oh yeah
> GB: Yeah. Here's the card. I will see you there in five minutes. Room 402.

And he just started laughing. Both of us did. I think it was my awkward bobbing around in my seat that was supposed to look like dancing that sent him over the edge. His people at the end were saying 'That's proper funny,' but they were also shocked. 'Gerard's not like that,' they said.

But the main thing they care about is the timings and how long the whole interview is going to take. I tend to enter the room, muck about for a minute, maybe a couple, and walk out, and they say: 'Oh is that it? Brilliant.' If that is it, they are normally happy.

But the other thing about this one is Gerard Butler's normally stern-faced heavies enjoyed it. I could hear them in the background sniggering like little school kids as *Soccer AM* brought out a side of him they had never seen before.

In fact the amount of times you hear them struggling to hold in their laughter at junkets is funny. After the initial shock at what they are seeing their star do, they get involved. I've lost count of the amount of times I've come out of a hotel room at a junket and been hugged or high-fived by Americans on the way out when beforehand they were being rude and looking down their noses at me. I get a real buzz out of that. It makes you happy when people tell you to come back.

I saw Gerard Butler recently at another junket and thought he would walk past and was never going to remember me. But he came up to me and was all 'Eh mate, how you doing? I didn't see our thing, was it good? A lot of people told me about it. Thanks a lot for that.'

I was surprised he felt the need to say thanks. 'No, thank you,' I said. 'No, no,' he replied, 'it is good to do things like that because people think I'm like this or that.'

I didn't really know what he meant and why he kept saying thanks. Later I realised he had been in the papers a lot due to some personal problems, which probably shape what people think about him. Just doing that little interview, he felt, helped show him in a different light. Although it was not the plan – I didn't actually know about his problems beforehand – it was nice of him to say. Obviously I wish him all the best too.

Another actor, Jim Carrey, I suspect didn't have to change quite as much to be the person who appeared in front of the *Soccer AM*. When I walked in, I was thinking he could be a funny guy like the one you see on screen, and he didn't disappoint. It was like when I met Hulk Hogan. He was screaming and roaring 'Hey man' all the time, just like he was whenever you would see him on TV and he was in Hulk Hogan wrestling mode.

Jim Carrey was making silly noises and pulling silly faces, just like most of the characters he plays in films do. I was thinking to myself: 'He can't be like that all the time, surely? It must take up so much energy.'

TV presenter Keith Lemon is similar. He was great with me but he was exactly like he is on TV, even when the cameras turn off. He was just playing Keith Lemon. Or maybe he was just being normal.

How do they do that? It is not like I go around all day spitting stupid lyrics at people all day. People are surprised when they meet me that I'm not what I'm like on TV.

Anyhow, Jim Carrey started off as he is in his films then we started talking about football after he worked out, like Nicole Scherzinger, what *Soccer AM* was all about. 'Who do you support?' he asked. 'Chelsea,' I replied. 'I follow Chelsea,' he said. 'I have been to Stamford Bridge a few times and when I went the atmosphere was amazing. Can you teach me a song?'

His PR people and the film junket people were saying, this is not part of the interview, but he was cool. 'Nah, nah, nah. Who cares about the schedule,' he shouted.

When you attend these junkets you usually get a warning just letting you know how much time you have for each interview. Normally I don't need anywhere the amount of time I'm given and I just tell the organisers to give the spare time to somebody else.

'No. It doesn't work like that,' is normally the response I get from some busybody. Really, I mean how difficult would that be to do?

This time it was five minutes per person, but I ended up staying in the room for about twenty minutes because he was trying to learn the 'Celery' Chelsea chant.

As soon as the celebrity says 'No, it's fine,' their people stand down and pander to their wishes. 'OK,

OK, if that's what you want,' or words to that effect. It's really pathetic.

Stupidly, the 'Celery' song was the first Chelsea song that came into my head to teach him. It is also probably one of the rudest.

'What? Is that really the song?' Jim Carrey said. I laughed 'Yeah,' but at the same time was thinking there is no way we can show this at 11 a.m. in the morning. But he said: 'Teach me it. You've got to teach me it.'

So I sat there for about five minutes just chanting 'celery, celery, celery'. Every now and then that thought from the Jean-Claude Van Damme interview would crop into my head – 'This is so bizarre'.

Anyway, he started learning the words and singing it. Then he got to the naughty bit. 'What? No, that can't be it,' he said. 'Yeah,' I said, a little sheepishly, 'it is.' 'That's amazing,' he laughed back at me.

Then the conversation took another weird turn. 'Tell me about your celery stories,' he asked. The first one I could think of was the time I went to the FA Cup Final and my uncle bought a massive bag of celery and we were in the bar beforehand lobbing celery everywhere.

Then he asked if he could come next time. There was only one answer. 'Yes Jim Carrey, you can come with us to Chelsea next time,' I said. What else was I supposed to tell this multi-award-winning actor when he asked to join me at a football match?

Now, his people were getting really annoyed. They were off camera frantically waving their arms and pointing at imaginary watches on their wrists, Sir Alex Ferguson-style.

I could see them mouthing 'Hurry up, hurry up'. He said: 'Nah, nah, nah, nah, nah. Tell me another one.' And that relaxes you because you know he is going to want to play along, and what he says goes.

While we were mucking about I hadn't even got to the question yet, so you can imagine what all the clock-watching junket people off camera were like. While I had Jim Carrey's permission though I knew I was fine to keep talking:

'Hi Jim I'm Tubes from *Soccer AM*, I've got One Question and One Question Only. It is, Jim Carrey, my back is really hairy... it is like I'm like Teen Wolf.'

Once I recovered from my sick lyrics, I just looked up and stared at him... for a long time.

> Jim Carrey: Wow. There is really nothing to say after that. I just wish you would cheer up man. Are you OK? I know CPR. You seem to be going up and down here. Losing contact with that part of yourself that holds the joy.
> T: Anyway, you are a really good bloke and I love you. You are one of my favourite actors. But I really want to be like you and be able to do your facial expressions. Could you give me some tips on how you do them, please?

Like most of the interview Jim Carrey's response was not what I was expecting as he basically showed me how to kill myself and then told me to do it.

'You've got visualise it,' he explained. 'Wet your finger

and pretend you've just stuck your finger into a plug
socket... ' He mimicked doing it and screwed up his
face and made a noise that sounded like a blender, which
was meant to be the sound he'd make if he was being
electrocuted.

Then I kept doing it and then he did. We were just going
back and forth, trying to out-electrocute ourselves and make
ridiculous faces. We had to put a warning on screen in the
show just to remind the kids at home not to copy Jim
Carrey's advice! Eventually I gave up and just started
staring at him.

> JC: Now I am trying to figure out what it is
> about you that is so special because I think
> you've been hurt. I can see that. Did Chelsea
> lose?
> T: No. No.
> JC: Oh OK. All right.
> T: Try again.
> JC: OK. You miss David Beckham?
> T: No. He played for Man United.
> JC: Oh OK ha-ha – I don't know the subtleties.
> OK, you miss Posh Beckham?
> T: No. She is a nice girl but I don't miss her.
> JC: Come on man? OK, well there is nowhere
> else to go but up from here. Seriously. Just
> kill yourself.

Inside I was cracking, but on the outside I was trying to
keep a straight face. It was hilarious. Another one of those

surreal, pinch yourself moments. Jim Carrey tells me 'You should kill yourself. Just kill yourself.' I have no idea why.

I said thanks and was ready to walk off but still he wasn't finished. He was loving it. He decided he wanted a stare-off. It was about 10–15 seconds but neither of us broke so I would say it was a draw.

Then when the cameras went off he just wanted to talk even more about football. He was asking me about everything – Frank Lampard, the songs, how long I had been going and how I got into Chelsea. I just thought: 'What a nice bloke.' I mean, why was he bothered about what I do?

He said: 'I just love the mentality of English football fans. It is like the army. You've got your army and you have the opposition and hate each other for 90 minutes and then afterwards everyone is friends again.' It was interesting to listen to.

'It's different in America,' he explained. 'Everyone is sitting there looking glum, drinking large drinks, getting a hot dog, walking in and out of the game. But for 90 minutes you guys are intense just staring at the pitch.' He actually did care. It was nice to have a proper chat with somebody after dealing with some stars who are a little bit fond of themselves.

At the end of the interview he just kept saying 'Amazing, amazing, that guy and that interview were amazing,' before he chanted me out by shouting 'Celery, Celery' at the top of his voice.

CHAPTER 10

THE ONE THAT SLIPPED THROUGH THE NET... AND MY BOY SWAAAAAAAAY

Like I have said, I'm a lucky, lucky fella. I've seen some cool things, met some amazing people and in general just had a right good laugh during my time so far at Sky and *Soccer AM*.

But there is one thing that has slipped through the net that I will just not give up on. Two words: Alesha 'she is so fit' Dixon (actually that's six, isn't it?).

One day, I am certain I will persuade her to go out with me. But for the time being, my attempts to get her to take me seriously and go out for a drink remain just a long-running joke on *Soccer AM*. Even after we went to never-seen-before lengths to try and get me a date with her.

Alesha Dixon loves *Soccer AM* and used to say it was her favourite programme. I suspect a big part of her love for the programme is because she could relate to a bad-boy rapper like me as she was the rapper in the girl group Mis-Teeq. She used to come on the show quite a lot and get everybody going with her really distinctive, loud laugh and obviously her stunning looks. Whenever she was on she would spend the whole show cracking up. For some reason she used to find me funny, and hopefully now still finds me mildly amusing, though I am sure it was more a case of her laughing at me rather than with me.

When I used to do the red-carpet stuff and before she got really famous, she always used to come running over, all excited and have a chat with us for *Soccer AM*. So it wasn't long before a running joke started going around the office that Tubes and Alesha Dixon loved each other.

The truth was, I fancied the pants off her and she didn't give two hoots about me (or so she tried to make out). But that doesn't matter. Let's just go with the rumour.

So one week my bosses at Sky had an idea: Alesha Dixon is coming on the show this weekend, so we will send Tubes for a makeover so he is looking his best for her.

And they got it sorted.

Someone pulled some strings and got in touch with William Hunt, in my eyes the top suit-maker on Savile Row, who loves his football and also does a lot of suits for the players, including teams' FA Cup Final suits (no, he didn't do that never-to-be-forgotten white suit Liverpool wore years back!).

He was more than happy to get involved. 'Bring him down to my shop, I'll get him all suited and booted,' he said.

THE ONE THAT SLIPPED... AND MY BOY SWAAAAAAAAAY

World-famous hairdresser Nicky Clarke was also very happy to sort out my barnet. In fact, it's down to Nicky that I've had a little bit more luck with the ladies since the barnet and woeful sideburns did one! And I needed some professional help if I was going to get a girl like Alesha Dixon. 'Bring him down to my salon and I will make him look good,' he promised.

All week there was this massive build-up ahead of Alesha Dixon's appearance on the show. I had the cameras following me around during the week for my makeover. They filmed me getting fitted up by William Hunt and then going to see Nicky Clarke and having all the foil stuff in my hair getting my highlights done.

We got a whole video package done and my mum has still kept it on our Sky box at home because by the end of the week I looked completely different. My hair was like it is now, but fresh-out-of-the-hairdresser styled. They put make-up on me. I had a mint suit on, too, and I walked out and Alesha Dixon was blown away. 'Wow, you look amazing,' she screeched. I was happy with that. 'Shall we just go now?' I said, with a cheeky smile, trying to strike while the iron – and I! – was hot. She started cracking up again and that chilled me out a bit.

I was really nervous before this one because we did such a big build-up but was trying my best to stay in control. I thought if I muck this one up I'm going to look like a right idiot.

Obviously it was rapping that first caught Alesha Dixon's attention so I wrote some extra special lyrics for the show. 'When I say Savile, you say Row, Savile, (audience) Row,

Savile, (audience) Row, Savile, (audience) Row, look at me now you can't say no.'

Everyone was up out of their seats roaring and cheering. I was buzzing partly because I didn't blow it like I did when Nadine Velazquez came on the show. Nicky Clarke and all the guys that had helped get me ready were there on the sofa, joining in too. It was probably the best reactions to a live question we've had.

After it all died down, Helen Chamberlain asked if I had a question, which was obviously for Alesha Dixon. 'Can I sit next to you?' I said, and everyone cracked up again. She said: 'Yes you can.'

So I spent the next part of the show sitting next to her with my arm around her, staring her up and down. Helen and Max Rushden were egging her on, asking her 'Will you go out with Tubes now, will you go out with Tubes now?' But that has not happened so I haven't quite broken her yet.

I haven't changed my appearance since because I actually looked pretty good and Alesha Dixon loved it. That has to go down as one of my favourite things I have done on the show. But I didn't go home with Alesha Dixon so I wasn't totally happy. I want to work with her too. Mis-Teeq are coming back so maybe I'll get my chance to do a little collaboration.

If you are reading this, Alesha (I know you were first in the queue for my book, I know it!), and you need a reference, just ask Sway. He will tell you I am made for the music industry. (Sway, if you are reading, and I know you are, just make some nonsense up for when she phones you for that reference. Stop laughing, mate – she will call!)

THE ONE THAT SLIPPED... AND MY BOY SWAAAAAAAAAY

My cousin Terry always used to bang on about this guy called Sway, years and years ago when the likes of Kano were coming through. I had heard a few bits of his music and I liked it. Then we used one of his songs on *Showboat* and decided we had to get him on. He was obviously quite decent, and in my eyes he is much more than decent.

Sway eventually came on the show and because he was a rapper I thought I would ask him the One Question and One Question Only. Rappers' union and all that. Just for a laugh, I asked him when he wants to collaborate and he said 'Whenever you want'. Everyone was cheering because it looked like I had finally got my big break and I was finally going to be on a rap tune.

At the end of show he came up to me and said 'I'm serious, by the way.' 'Really?' I said, as I had only been mucking around. 'Nah, nah, nah, nah, nah,' Sway said. 'I reckon we can do something good.' We swapped numbers but I still thought that would be the end of it. He would forget about it and was just saying it to humour me.

A couple of months later I was sitting in the editing suite putting together a *Showboat* package and my phone rang. 'Unknown number' was flashing on the screen. A little confused, I picked up.

'Hello Tubes, it's Sway,' says the voice on the other end of the phone. Oh no, not another Slash-style wind-up, I'm thinking.

'I've written a song for us,' the voice on the other end of the phone said. 'It's called "The Fatso Dance".'

'What are you trying to say?' I asked him.

'Nah, nah, nah. It's not about you,' he said 'it's about

how you stretch and warm up to get fit. I've written the song, come down to my studio and hear it.'

I still wasn't convinced and was certain it was a wind-up. I told people at Sky and they told me to go for it because they reckoned it would be funny. Probably because they thought it might be yet another opportunity to rip it out of me if I made myself look like a plank.

I turned up at the address. It was a studio. Sway was there. Maybe this wasn't a wind-up after all. And all I had to do was 'muck around, just go for it' while Sway was singing and his little brother TJ was doing the dance.

So we start filming and in between him rapping, I was chucking in the odd cheek wobble, random catchphrase or weird noise. I was pretty certain that my strange outbursts were actually ruining Sway and little TJ's hard work but Sway loved it and wanted to release it.

Zoo magazine turned up to the video shoot too, so there was a double-page spread of me and Sway doing the tune. It was crazy. My boss at Sky/*Soccer AM*, Rob Wakeling, liked the song so wanted Sway to come on the last show of the season and perform it. 'Oh no,' I thought. I was OK being Peter the Test Tube Baby and the Tubes, but was absolutely bricking it about doing a live rap performance. Why did they want to put me through this? We did it anyway and it was funny with TJ on dance duty. We got Chris Kamara involved too, dressed as a gangster rapper.

From there Sway and I became quite close. Not as close as I wanted to be with Alesha Dixon, obviously, but still close.

With Tim Lovejoy gone from *Soccer AM* by this stage,

Sway decided to step into his shoes and come up with ideas for things for me to do, and he reckoned I was perfect for a role in the video for his song 'Level Up'. 'Great' I thought. 'I'll get to see how it all works behind the scenes,' and stuff like that.

But it turned out to be a bit more than that. I turned up and he showed me the storyboard for the video. I was in pencil sketch and looked like a ghost, and I said: 'What is all this?'

'You are the main face of the video,' Sway said back to me. Totally straight-faced too, so I knew he wasn't messing about. 'Your character has won the lottery. Just do what you want.'

I just thought I'd have a walk-on part at best. I wasn't expecting to do the whole thing and be the main character in the video. It was a complete shock. I had to double check I was supposed to be in all those scenes. 'You're in everything,' he said.

Given there was a scene in a club where I was celebrating my lottery win with loads of fit girls around me I am not sure that was the best advice. But no, muck around on the dance floor, look at all the fit girls all around me was all I had to do. Sa-weeeet!

There was another part of the video when I am filthy rich after winning the lottery and we were walking up the red carpet to some posh do and I started bringing out the Robot Dance. Why not? I didn't know what I was I doing to be fair. Sway said do what you want so I did. While we were filming he was just shouting 'that's perfect, perfect, perfect.'

And it all worked out. We had a great laugh filming it

that day and it ended up making the Top 10 and has got millions of hits on YouTube, making it one of his best ever tracks (certainly my favourite ha-ha). Sway was over the moon, obviously.

I can't take a huge amount of credit for the success of 'Level Up'. It was his idea and his brilliant lyrics... I just brought the Oscar-winning performance to it ha-ha

I think he is brilliant. He is an absolute genius. I love his lyrics and he changes his style all the time. It is people like him, who are so, so talented, that should be getting much more recognition than they do. But these days people seem to be obsessed by all the boy bands and *X-Factor* performers. Even going back, you look at people like MC Hammer and Vanilla Ice who I don't think are very good. Yet they make millions. I don't get it. I just don't get it.

Anyhow, it was a long old day doing that video. I thought I might be needed for an hour maybe but I was there for nearly 24. We started at 7 a.m. in the morning and finished at 3 a.m. the next morning. I got to live the dream, though, like when I found out Sway had hired loads of Ferraris and Porsches all for me, the lottery winner. Some of the girls as well – wow!

For the red-carpet and robot scene, because by that stage in the video story I had won the lottery I had to wear a suit to look like a man with money. That was all fine, except for the fact that the one they gave me didn't fit. I was much heavier than I am now. I had some rascal shoes on, too. Ridiculous, shiny things. Sway looked cool as, and I looked like a scruff. Like someone who was trying to look smart but had got it all wrong.

THE ONE THAT SLIPPED... AND MY BOY SWAAAAAAAAAY

I said to the costume guys: 'If I had won the lottery, I wouldn't be wearing this clobber.' What I needed was my William Hunt suit. I would have loved that. 'Seriously, guys, if I won the lottery I wouldn't be wearing this,' I said.

I tried begging to Sway because surely he would want the main attraction looking his absolute best. Nope! No luck there either. 'Don't worry about it. It will be all right,' he said.

The costume people were wetting themselves because I couldn't fit into it. It felt like another wind-up. I looked like The Penguin from *Batman*. Or just an idiot. Sway was crying with laughter. There was no other option, though. I had to just do it, in that suit.

When I was doing the robot, that was literally the only move I could do because the suit was so tight. The trousers didn't fit, the shirt didn't fit, the jacket was too small. I just looked like a massive doughnut. I was even a little worried the suit would split. It was ridiculous.

You'd never know it from the video, though. It looks fine and I managed to cover it up.

The other guys in the video were trained actors. They were asking me what else have I been in and stuff like that. They recognised me from *Soccer AM* but thought I did acting as well. Obviously I said no, because I don't. 'Come on?' they said. 'Honestly I don't,' I said. 'I am just being me. Just being stupid.' I must be a natural, or I'm just good at mucking about!

I've spoken to Sway quite a bit recently about doing some more stuff together – I guess it's a case of watch this space. You see, Alesha... this is what you're missing out on! So here's my number... So call me maybe?

CHAPTER 11

COME AND HAVE A GO IF YOU THINK YOU'RE HARD ENOUGH (YOU PROBABLY ARE)

One of the best post-interview reactions was never ever captured on camera for your viewing pleasure. And, for once, the fact an interview didn't go to plan was nothing to do with me. That makes this story a really tough one for me to tell. Even after all these years I still haven't got over it and have only just forgiven the cameraman I had with me on the day.

If it wasn't for the sake of this book I am not sure I would be mentally ready to retell the story of the day Jason Statham made me look like an absolute idiot – only to crack and pretty much tell me I am the greatest thing since sliced bread... once the cameras had stopped rolling.

That was the best part of the day because the interview itself was a weird one. I walked in for his junket before the release of his film *The Transporter* and I thought: 'This guy is going to be a top bloke or completely the opposite.' I just wasn't sure at all.

Also, when you see how people are perceived in the media and you see them walking around town or pictured in the papers giving it a bit, you expect to meet that person. He was either going to be an absolute doughnut or a top bloke. No middle ground.

When I entered the room and he seemed like he was heading for the 'top bloke' end of the scale, I thought 'Ah ledge'. He was nice, welcoming and polite – 'Ehhhhh, alwight, 'ow ah ya, mate,' in that stereotypical Londoner, film-hardman accent of his. 'Ah yeah, this is *Socc'ah AM* is it? Yeah I 'ave 'eard of it, yeah, yeah, yeah.' Given what I was thinking beforehand I was cool with that.

After the usual introductions I stuck the crucial question on him; 'What is the best scene you have ever seen in a film?' Not the most taxing question for somebody whose job was all about films, you would think. But he didn't seem impressed:

Jason Statham: I don't want to answer that.
Tubes: Oh.

He carried on for some time insisting that he was not going to answer the question.

JS: I don't know.
T: Oh go on.
JS: No.

So we just sat in silence for ages. Then he crushed my hopes once and for all by making it clear I wasn't going to get an answer. 'No. I'm not answering it,' he said.

We carried on chatting about something else. And then for ages we were just looking at each other, having another one of my stare-offs, blank looks on both of our faces. Then time ran out and I said: 'Okay, thanks for your time.' 'No problem. No problem,' he said.

Usually when you go to a junket there are two cameras. One on you and one on the celebrity, already set up when you walk in the room. This time it was a one-camera shoot so I had to take my own cameraman. But the cameraman (who, because I am such a nice guy, will remain nameless) had got a bit trigger-happy and switched his camera off as soon as we said our goodbyes.

Now, normally the best or only reactions happen when I walk off and they have time to reflect on the dipstick they've just been talking to, normally pulling a confused face, or just calling me all sorts of names!

So when, after Dopey Balls switched off the camera, Jason Statham proper creased up into a ball of laughter I was buzzing, thinking this could be up there with the best. His reaction basically saved the day. 'That was the best [bleep] interview I've ever had. That was [bleep] genius. What a load of [bleep].'

During the interview, I was confused. I didn't know if he had the hump. Was I going to get some of his *Transporter*-style, kung-fu treatment that he dishes out in the film?

But he just kept shouting '[Bleep] brilliant, mate, [bleep]

come here you [really badly needed bleep for a really bad swear word],' and he gave me a massive hug.

Job done, get in, T Unit! But... I turned to the cameraman, who I expected to look almost has happy as me.

The look on his face said it all. I knew exactly what he was about to say. 'I turned the camera off,' he confessed. That meant all you lovely viewers got to see was Jason Statham appearing to be Charlie Big Spuds, when he was actually mucking around and playing with my emotions the whole time.

So me and Jason Statham tag-teamed up and gave the cameraman a master class in karate that Bruce Lee would have been proud of. Actually, that's a little porkie. We didn't. What really happened was I just got a proper sulk on and left with a face like thunder.

I was fuming on the way home. Absolutely fuming. Still, the other camera recorded Jason's laugh. The sound of it, anyway. But you can't see it, because the camera was pointing at me. You can hear him cracking up but you can't see it, making the audio no use whatsoever.

The journey back to Sky Towers was fun. All the way back all I was thinking was 'Thanks for nothing, mate.' Poor guy, all he could keep repeating was: 'Sorry Tubes, I'm so sorry.' After ten minutes, I chilled out and told Dopey Balls not to worry about it. I'm not one to hold a grudge. What's the point? Once something has happened you can't change it, can you? You just need to carry on regardless. If he does it again, though, my special move – the 'one-inch punch' – will be out in full force, with no hesitation.

COME AND HAVE A GO IF YOU THINK YOU'RE HARD ENOUGH

It is a tough job judging the real personalities of the hard men from the film world. Because they look one way on the screen you just expect them to be the same. You don't know if people are actually all right.

It was like that with Vinny Jones. I had never met the guy but he tweeted me out of the blue, saying 'All right son?' I have still never met him, to this day. But he tweeted me. 'This is not Vinny Jones,' I thought. But I clicked on the message and it looked like it really did come from the official Vinny Jones, so I replied.

Tubes: Yeah I'm alright mate, you?
Vinny Jones: Yeah I'm alright. I miss England.
T: Yeah, but Hollywood ain't bad is it?
VJ: Yeah but I'm missing the football and all that.

It was weird, having a conversation with Vinny Jones on Twitter when I have never met the guy before. It can't be because he needs more followers because he's got millions already.

VJ: Come out and do an interview with me.
T: All right.

I tried to get it sorted out with something else that we couldn't get sorted out. We wanted to get a Hollywood United crossbar challenge but they couldn't warrant me just going out there for an interview. Which was quite annoying, but at the same time quite understandable. It would cost thousands of pounds for a five-minute interview!

I would've loved the chance to have a jolly up with Vinny Jones in Hollywood, though. I'd just give it large to people and then stand behind him when it all kicks off... ha-ha. Screen hardmen Tamer Hassan and Danny Dyer are a couple of others who are friends of the show.

Danny Dyer is exactly what he's like on TV in real life. All 'Yeah alwight mate, alwight mate'. He's a top bloke and also very funny. I have met him loads of times. He's been on *Soccer AM* a good few times. Tamer Hassan is a bit of a geezer as well. Just like he is on TV.

Another one is Liam Gallagher. He literally does do that funny, loping walk that you see him do on TV. And he is well in your face. He came up to me once and in his strong Mancunian accent just shouted at me: 'Ask me a question.'

'What's the best goal Man City have ever scored?' was the best I could come up with on the spot. 'That's a not very good question!' (or words to that effect) he barked back... and walked off! Nice one Liam, nice to meet you too pal... ha-ha.

Noel Gallagher is completely different and one of the coolest and funniest guys I have ever met. He just swags around, oozing cool. Two things stick out with me about the great man himself. Once he came on *Soccer AM* and it was around Christmas time and we gave him a present for him and his children.

In a flash and before he had even held it he said: 'Please tell me it's James Blunt's head.' It was funny as – not the view of myself or *Soccer AM*, obviously, but very funny all the same. The other one is a story he actually told me... about me.

COME AND HAVE A GO IF YOU THINK YOU'RE HARD ENOUGH

One of the best nights I ever had was when me and some of the *Soccer AM* boys were invited to Noel's 40th birthday party (clang). To this day I still can't believe I was invited. Anyhow, let's just say the occasion, and free drinks, got to me a little bit. Apparently as I left the club at about 4 a.m., I realised I was in Soho Square, Central London.

I lived in Cobham. Roughly an hour away in a car or six hours on foot. I certainly didn't fancy the 'on-foot' option, so I was stumbling around looking for a cab. Noel Gallagher told me I walked up to what, in my state, I thought was a cab... but was actually a stretch limo:

Tubes: You going Cobham pal?
Cabbie: Nah mate, I'm actually Noel's personal driver.
T: No worries, can you go via Cobham though?
C: You're having a laugh, aren't you mate?

Then he drove off. Apparently Noel was in the back of the limo with his now wife, creasing up.

He never lets me forget that incident, not that I could remember it in the first place. Anyhow, I went off on one there. Back to some of the hardmen I've spoken to. That's not to say Liam and Noel Gallagher aren't double hard, of course.

One man you don't mess with when he tells you something is Sylvester Stallone. I was dead excited to meet him. This was Sly Stallone, aka Rocky. I wanted to meet him badly. So I got my rap ready and then got told I couldn't do it, his people being over-protective yet again, so it turned into a serious interview.

That is maybe what led to the footballer interviews and me finally getting a bit more serious. Sylvester Stallone might have been the reason I changed... just about six years later. I was just going to ask him a question but it became... 'Hi Sly, I'm Tubes from *Soccer AM*,' and I was about to launch into the usual rap but then I had to remember I wasn't allowed to do it.

I ended up just interviewing him normally. I felt a little bit like Jeremy Paxman. It was weird. And it didn't seem that funny to me, though apparently it was to people watching it, or at least that's what they said (as they laughed behind my back).

The second time, he let me rap to him: 'Hi Sly, I'm Tubes from *Soccer* AM. I've got One Question and One Question Only. You're from the USA, You're so hard you make them pay, oooh, oooh, oooh, oooh, Rambo style.'

> Sylvester Stallone: Now we're talking. Well I... he is a modern-day Frankenstein. A guy who went to war, came back, nobody appreciated him, America built him and now he is...

He was waffling on so I had to cut him off.

> T: That wasn't my question...
> SS: It wasn't? Well that was the longest, chirpiest, weirdest question I have ever heard but I'm gonna give you a second shot.
> T: Thanks
> SS: Go for it my man.

T: You're a great actor and I love you. But who is harder? You or Arnie [Arnold Schwarzenegger]?

SS: Arnie.

T: Really?

SS: Yeah. I have to admit because this guy can take... actually, it's one thing to lift weights and it's another to... but Arnold can take the pressure of being asked thousands of questions and interrupted and being bombarded by people [as a politician] and I can't handle it. He is tough.

T: You are pretty buff though, aren't you?

SS: Well, you know, muscles are easy. Brains? He's got the right brains to deal with the everyday pressure of being a local governor, which he is.

T: Cool. That was a really good answer.

Luckily what he didn't see was me dropping off as he rambled on. He really did go on. And on. And on. And on. The camera that was focused on me nabbed me but I have no idea how he didn't see it. Thank God he didn't. He is Rocky and he would've knocked me the hell out!

TUBES EXTRA

SOME CHRISTMAS-THEMED RAPS

Most share their Chrimbo with a big fat turkey, I keep it real and have beef jerky, Ooooo times are hard.

I love Chrimbo and pulling a cracker, mum gave me sprouts so I had to sack her, Ooooo new chef please.

He's a top man, his name is Santa, last year he left my mince pies, Ooooo poor banter.

It's Christmas and it's time to be merry, get me the mistletoe and Katie Perry, Ooooo fit.

It's Christmas Day, and I am jolly, mum screwed up, she got me a Border collie, Ooooo I wanted a bulldog.

TUBESOLOGY

It's Christmas night so it's time for charades, Nan button it, no I'm not playing cards.

CHAPTER 12

I'M A BIG FAN OF MR BEAN... I GOT DONE BY PROFESSOR GREEN

I wasn't so lucky when Professor Green came on *Soccer AM*. In fact, I was put right back in my box.

You might have noticed that I can spit a lyric or two. However, when Professor Green was a guest I got well and truly schooled. Most weeks there is nothing for anyone to compare my lyrical skills to, but it seemed that Professor Green had had enough and wanted to show the world how it was really done. He was really keen, in fact, and was the one who set up our rap battle, which has gone down in *Soccer AM* history. I knew there was a good chance it was going to end horribly for me because he was the one who requested it. You don't ask to challenge someone unless you are pretty confident you'll beat them.

He called up Trevor Giess, *Soccer AM*'s music man at the time and two-times *Soccer AM* dance-off champion, and said: 'I'm coming on the show this week and want to have a rap battle with Tubes. Live on the show.'

At first I thought it was a wind-up and didn't take it seriously. I mean, why would a rapper as talented as Professor Green want a rap battle with me? What was there to be gained? I was *Soccer AM*'s resident rapper, but this was Professor Green. He was a pro – literally – and I was an amateur, nearer budget. He didn't need to be doing that.

Still, that didn't stop me checking out the opposition, just in case. I wish I hadn't bothered. I went on YouTube and found some of his freestyle videos. There was only one word for them – sickening.

His speed of thought was scary – as I was about to find out first hand. I could sit down and come up with a silly little rap but he was coming up with clever stuff. What I do is not clever in the slightest. Though I did think my second response against Professor Green was quite good. In the circumstances it might actually be one of the best raps I have ever come up with.

Watching him in action was good preparation in some ways. But in others it wasn't. It made me think, 'Christ, what have I got myself into?' or, more accurately, 'Look how Trev has stitched me up.'

Watching the Professor was like watching something out of *Eight Mile*. He would literally just grab the mic and kill people lyrically. He is a top bloke too, by the way. An absolute geezer. He used to go to all the underground clubs. I suppose in some ways he is quite similar to Eminem. A white rapper, who used to just go to all the clubs and destroy people, something I tend to do in the country pubs of Surrey. This is what I was up against.

And the closer it got to the Saturday, the more I was getting worried about it. Because I knew what I was coming up against I planned my first response to his opening shot...

> Professor Green: I'm the Professor, the one that you don't wanna test, Tubes is about as smart as the Soccerette.

The studio erupts. Laughter, raucous applause from everyone. Except me. I'm bricking it even more. But I didn't have time to worry about that, I had to hit him with my response...

> Tubes: You think you are lyrical waxy [I picked my phone out of my pocket and pretended to answer it] hang on a minute (down the phone), yeah OK, you might as well go because I've got you a taxi!

The studio erupted again. Phew. I had held my own. I'm sure I even heard someone shout 'One–nil Tubes'. I was ready to take that. But then he came back at me again. I was not expecting this.

> PG: Although I seem cool, I can be cruel, Tubes got kicked out of the gene pool.

More laughter. Again. At my expense. I was in a real pickle here. But my weird brain clicked into gear and I came up with something to get myself out of a hole. And I have absolutely no idea where my second reply came from either.

> T: Bananaman or Super Ted, I won this battle,
> I'm going back to bed.

Everyone went nuts again. And with that I walked off. Outta there. Or 'outy', as Big Den might say. I walked off at about the same speed I did when I needed a quick exit after fluffing my lines to Nadine Velazquez.

Mark Watson and Dion Dublin were also on the show. Everyone in the studio was going mental. Dion Dublin was one of the guests with his Dube instrument and was banging on it like a madman. I got a massive buzz off it.

'Bananaman or Super Ted'... what on earth? But, please forgive me, I literally had seven or eight seconds to think of something and that was all that came to mind. If you look at my face you can see I'm defeated after his second lyric. He has killed me and I was going to bottle it. I just wasn't expecting to have to come back with a second. But everyone was shouting at me, 'You won, you won,' so I'll take that.

The truth is, the only reason I won was because I bottled it and chucked the microphone at him before walking off. If I didn't do a runner he would have just carried on. And on. And on. And on. And left me looking very stupid. I knew I had to get out of there ASAP once I had delivered that second lyric, before I ran out of things to say.

I think it was the surprise factor of the rap battle as much as anything else that caught people out and made it go down as one of the most memorable things to happen on the show. Professor Green still thanks me for doing it to this day and says so many people have come up to him and said, 'Your rap battle with Tubes was immense,' or words along those lines. But it will never be done again. Last time he came on he said: 'We're not doing a rap battle this time, are we?'

I said: 'No, no, we're not,' relieved a little that he didn't want to go toe to toe, lyric to lyric again. He thought it had been done and we didn't need to go over old ground again.

It was like when Serge 'Serge' Pizzorno from Kasabian scored *that* goal in our end-of-show game *On The Road To Wembley*, when he flicked it up and volleyed it straight into the hole.

Serge has got even more fame because of that goal and says he often has people coming up to him asking if it was him who scored *that* goal. But he won't try and do it again. He says 'it has been done,' and so he doesn't take the kick at the end game any more whenever he comes on the show, because he reckons he doesn't need to.

Professor Green thought the same about our rap battle. On the last show of the 2011/12 season they showed the clip, we had a laugh about it but that was it. Helen, as she does, was trying to goad him and wind him up, whispering: 'Tubes beat you, Tubes beat you,' trying to get him to do it again. But he said: 'I'm not going to do it again. It's done.'

I also saw Professor Green at the V Festival, which was quite a funny story. Me and Fenners went along and it turned out to be one of the best and booziest days of my life. Noel Gallagher had sorted myself and Fenners out so we could go and chill with him and his high-flying birds there. We finished *Soccer AM*, caught the train to Chelmsford and as we were walking there a blacked-out Mercedes drove alongside us.

The window winds down. Professor Green sticks his head out. 'Oiiiii oiiiii boys,' he shouts out the window. I put my hand out to shake his but just as I did the car jolted forward. I'm thinking 'Are you having a wind-up?'

His hand was still there so I went again and the car jolted forward again. Stupidly, I kept offering my hand and the car kept jolting forward and we ended up doing this routine all the way down the road. So 2–0 Pro Green!

Devlin is another top rapper in the mould of Professor Green that we've had on the show. He is immense. Wow. So good. So talented. Wiley, he is also a brilliant rapper we've had on the show. But he blew us out last time we invited him in. He sent a text to Devlin 'Dev' Tagoe, my mate at work, on the morning of the show that said 'Bruv, I'm not coming. Not leaving my house. It's too cold.'

To be fair it was freezing. I remember when I had to jump in the cab outside my house, it was ridiculously cold. 'You are joking, aren't you?' Dev replied. Another text came back. 'Nah. It's too cold.' He didn't turn up. That was genuinely his excuse.

It was a shame because the one time we got him on I thought he was one of the best guests we've ever had. I asked him my One Question and One Question Only: 'You mentioned earlier in your chat you are scared of spiders. What else are you scared of?' He just went, completely straight-faced: 'Immigration. Yeah bruv. Immigration.'

Everyone was in fits of laughter. Must admit I wasn't expecting that reply so all I could manage was: 'Okay.'

There was another rapper. He is also an actor in the film *Sweeney Todd*. The infamous Plan B. He turned up at the studio one morning.

He was talking to the girl at work who greets all the guests. She later told me he asked her: 'This is the show with that rapper fella?' 'Yeah, Tubes,' she said. 'Ah yeah, yeah, that's right,' he said. 'I like him, I like him, he's not all there is he?' was Plan B's assessment of me. Many people would say he is spot on!

Then he saw me and said 'Yeah, yeah, yeah, it's you innit?' I didn't know what he was talking about. 'Nah, you're funny, you're funny. Your lyrics are so bad, they're good.' It's funny to think that on a show about football, the one thing he remembered was the comedy/awful rapper, but I'll take it. He kept his glasses on during the show.

Because I am the closest *Soccer AM* has got to a rapper there is extra pressure on me when the real big-time rappers come on the show. And D12's appearance was another occasion when the spotlight was right on me. They were big intimidating guys and not to be messed with. They've worked with the likes of Eminem, so know what a proper rapper is.

Because of their status as extra-special guests I pulled in some help for an extra-special performance – my brother Andrew, or Big Ange as he is more commonly known – a two-man rap.

Big Ange was dressed up like me, black shirt and dark trousers, and at the time had shambolic hair like his big bro:

TUBESOLOGY

Tubes: I rap fast.

Big Ange: Well I rap slow.

T: We are the best rappers.

A: So you might as well gooooo.

Both: Oh, you know.

I thought we pulled it off. They all sat there and laughed. And laughed and laughed. And laughed a little bit more. It was one of those slow, deep laughs. They might as well have just said 'Who are these jokers?'

'They look like two Catholic priests,' was former D12 member Bizarre's assessment of our performance and appearance. Kuniva went further, though I am not sure who he was digging out, when he said: 'It's like a before-and-after shot.' I think he was saying Big Ange was the before!

Anyhow, I got them back by asking them if they make the noise I do when I drop the cheek wobble. You should have seen them squirming on the sofas as they all bottled it!

Obviously I don't take this whole rapping thing seriously. That's why I'm not ashamed of doing something in front of some of these big names. I never look at them and think, 'Oh it's D12,' or, 'Oh it's Akon.'

Speaking of Akon, he came on the show and was brilliant. He is a really clever bloke, articulate and well spoken. And I'll never forget his answer to my One Question and One Question Only: 'You're a great rapper and a real nice guy. What I want to know is, who is the greatest rapper ever?'

With about one second's thought he said 'I would probably say Eminem. Definitely say Eminem. Coz you gotta think about the obstacles he faced getting in. He came from a whole other culture. Literally, mastered it, outsold everybody and then did every kind of record you could imagine. A comedy record, party record, sexy record, drama record, theatrical record. He can take any topic and make a song out of it. I haven't seen any other artist that can do that.'

You could tell everybody thought 'Wow. Akon is saying Eminiem is the best rapper ever?' 'The guy is a genius,' he said.

My meeting with another big name from the States, Flo Rida, was also memorable – but this time for all the wrong reasons. It started off bad and then went downhill from there, when Flo Rida didn't remember who I was. I had actually met him before he came on the show at the MOBO Awards, six months earlier – not that he remembered! So I can't have made that much of an impression on him.

Helen Chamberlain said: 'You've met Tubes before at the MOBO Awards, yep?' His face was blank. He didn't have a Scooby. It was getting a bit awkward. Actually, it was really awkward. I had bowled onto the set thinking, 'Big Flo Rida knows me, he's my mate,' and the rest of the crew were stirring things up. 'Of course you do, Flo Rida, of course you remember Tubes.' He was just laughing because he genuinely had no idea who I was.

Helen teed me up again, as she loves doing when there is someone I might be a little nervous speaking to on the show. 'There's Flo Rida here today Tubes. You must be cacking ya pants?' she said patronisingly. 'Yeah. I'm bricking it, yeah,' I said. There was no point lying.

'You don't happen to remember Tubes do you by any chance? He mumbled something at you before you went in to the MOBO Awards.'

Flo Rida shakes his head.

Tubes: 'Course ya do.'

He shook his head again. Just sat there looking totally baffled.

Helen: Don't worry about it. You've got One Question and One Question Only, who is it for?
T: Flo Rida
H: Oh yeah, of course it is.

So I go to introduce my question with a Flo Rida-inspired rap... but managed to totally forget the lyrics to maybe his most famous song ever, 'Low': 'You go low, low, low, low, this is my flow, flow, flow, flow – cheers – I gotta go, go, go, go.'

I completely messed up the rap I'd prepared, and this time there was no coming back.

I didn't want a date with Flo Rida like I did with Nadine Velazquez so I just walked off set without even asking the question. It was the first time I'd ever done that. He was cracking up, everyone else was cracking up too, so in some ways it was still funny. I was just the only one not laughing. 'He bottled it. Totally bottled it. For the first time in history!' Helen said, almost sounding like she enjoyed my suffering.

I had better luck with 50 Cent. I was bricking it for a

different reason when I rocked up for his *Righteous Kill* junket. I was convinced he would be proper gangster. And with good reason, too, I thought. After all, this is a guy who has been shot loads of times, including a bullet in the face. He's clearly not someone you mess around with.

When I met his people they only added to the impression I had. They were what I would call, proper aggro. Really moody and looking at me like 'What are you doing here'.

I'd worked myself up into such a state about it that when he turned out to be all right I was really buzzing. Wow. It was a great feeling. A proper tough guy who had been shot nine times, got in the spirit of the interview and just took me in.

I reckon it was the lyrics that did it:

Tubes: Hi 50 I'm Tubes from *Soccer AM*. I've got One Question and One Question Only. You're 50 Cent and I've got lyrics that you can rent [cheek wobble], T-t-t-tuuubees unit. You are great bloke and one of the best rappers in the world. But I want to be like you and I want to be in the G-Unit.

50 Cent: [Biiiggg puff of the cheeks] I don't know. Maybe we gotta get somebody in here. Maybe a stylist, a barber.

T: What's up with my hair?

50: We gotta fix it up and change it around a little bit. We gotta get you some jewellery and gold teeth.

T: Proper blinging!

50: Ha-ha! You crazy man. I don't know. I don't

know what will make you fit in with the group.
What do you think would help?

T: I've got gangsta lyrics.

50: You've got gangsta lyrics?

T: Yeah.

50: See that thing you do with ya mouth?

So I did it again. It's a like a party piece. It comes out at any opportunity.

> 50: We might be able to market that. That might
> work. That could be your signature sound. We
> gotta be creative, we will come up with
> something.

And then we made up a stupid spud-style gangster hand-shake to complete my initiation into G-Unit.

What a top man he was. I met him again a second time the following year at his junket for the film *Dead Man Running*, which also featured Danny Dyer and Tamer Hassan. Loads of people were left frustrated as their planned interviews got pulled.

Fortunately, being a bit of weirdo worked in my favour. He remembered me from last time and I was one of the only people he was up for speaking to. And he was more than happy to give me some more tips to push me closer to getting that big break:

Tubes: All right 50, I'm Tubes from *Soccer AM*. I've got One Question and One Question Only. You are 50 Cent, I'm in love with Clark Kent [rips open shirt to reveal hairy chest], Suuuuuuperman!

50 Cent: I think you should try and shave that. It will do good for your love life. If you can get some of your hair off the girls might like you a little better.

T: It's sweet innit?

50: It's interesting because it looks like you have shaved the neck down to your chest because around your neck is clean and then you have got a little circle.

T: You're a top bloke and as you've just seen I'm one of the greatest rappers ever. But I have not been signed up to a record label yet. So what more can I do?

50: You need to figure out how we can make this happen. I think the problem is your image.

T What's wrong with my image?

50: The hair, the hair. It's kinda like Teenwolf. Maybe take the hair off and come back with a different vibe.

T: I thought it was pretty gangster.

50: It's kinda creepy actually. We just need to figure out how to get the hair off your chest or to keep your shirt closed when you actually say what you're trying to say because people can't concentrate on that when they look at you and see the hair.

T: I just want to rap for a living. I haven't got much of a chance, have I?

50: Nah, nah, I'm not gonna lie to you. We need to get you some jewellery. Some baseball hats and you got to get your story straight.

T: I love you man... [to the camera] What a man.

As you can see he was on good form. Once the cameras stopped rolling he said, 'I remember you from last time so I wanted to do an interview with you and you've perked me up.'

I actually took on one of his tips and shaved my chest. I haven't gone down the bling route, though. Yet! I've cut my hair too and I have had a bit of success with the ladies since. I'm not sure whether that's down to 50 Cent or my natural charm.

He was one of the biggest differences between my expectations and the reality. Because when you hear someone has been shot, I thought he was going to be all 'I'm a gangster rapper, I don't laugh and I don't need to talk to you idiots from the media,' and deadly serious all the time. But he was brilliant. Such a nice bloke and actually spoke quite well. When you see his music videos and all the swearing and aggressiveness, the guy I actually met was the complete opposite. And for him to say he wanted to speak to me again because he enjoyed it the first time meant a lot.

When the video cut off, I was still in the room and he was saying: 'Yep, that was great fun, love it, I enjoyed speaking to you. Superman, you're not Superman though are you? I love it though, it's funny.' It was amazing. What a top bloke.

It's weird because you sit there, pinching yourself a little, thinking, 'Wow this is 50 Cent'. Beforehand he'd just said, 'Do what you want, make me laugh.' And he played along. Reckon it would be a right laugh if he joined me and Colin Farrell on our night out.

I have saved the best and most iconic rapper who deserves a mention until last. He was also one of my heroes, who I got to meet thanks to *Soccer AM*.

If you're a white rapper, Vanilla Ice is *the* man, so there was only one answer when I was asked if I could go down and meet him. Growing up on the mean streets of Cobham as a white rapper, Eminem wasn't around, so it was always about Vanilla Ice for me. What he has done for rap and white rappers has changed the world really.

I met him when he was over here doing *Dancing on Ice* at Wembley Arena. Just like Slashgate, I took some food props with me when I went to go and see Vanilla Ice (Lavvers could you get me a bag of rice please, mate?) and drop some lyrics:

'Hi Vanilla Ice, I'm Tubes from *Soccer AM*. I've got One Question and One Question Only. You're a top man, you're Vanilla Ice, I'm hungry... I need some rice, rice, rice, baby,' and spilt the rice out of pockets all over the ice rink. Cue looks of horror from Torvill and Dean! Vanilla Ice played along and was trying to teach me how to do his hand sign, but said I ended up looking like Spock, this time, because I couldn't do it properly.

It was a dream of mine to have a rap battle with Vanilla Ice but he wasn't interested. I think he knew I have sicker lyrics than him and he must've been scared. He was trying to take his ice-skating seriously so he seemed all consumed by that and didn't want to go old skool with me. We just had a chat, one question, I gave him a cuddle and left. Another one off the list. Vanilla Ice, what a man.

CHAPTER 13

WRESTLEMANIA!

I don't mind a challenge in this job but, to put it simply, Mickey Rourke took the biscuit.

I didn't know too much about him before I met the American actor so I did my usual pre-interview research. And two things kept cropping up, time and time again: bad boy and ladies' man. I thought it was an American version of me (then I woke up).

I'd heard the usual scare stories from the boring lot, telling me he wasn't playing ball or he wasn't on good form. But history told me not to pay much attention as there is always a chance that doing something different for *Soccer AM* will lead to a different reaction from the star we go to see. Not with Mickey Rourke.

I couldn't get the 'bad boy' and 'ladies' man' expectations out of my head when I went to meet him at the Savoy

Hotel in London to speak to him at his junket for *The Wrestler*. When I pushed open the door, what I saw was one of the strangest things I have ever seen: him sat in the middle of the hotel room, with a dog on his lap, surrounded by a thick cloud of smoke. Somewhere in the middle of it was Micky Rourke.

'Hey man,' he said, in a voice that was so deep it sounded like he hardly had the energy to speak. 'Si'down.' I have never walked into a hotel room where the interviewee is smoking. And sat with a dog on their lap.

I asked his people what was going on. 'He won't let the dog go,' I was told pretty bluntly. I wasn't too fussed about the dog. The dog could stay. It would be a first on *Soccer AM*. I was more concerned about the smoking.

Mickey Rourke said: 'What's the problem?' 'Well it's a morning show,' I explained to him, 'and you are smoking.' He shrugged his shoulders. 'You either do the question or you don't do the question... Up to you,' he said. Charming!

I asked the question anyway, even though I know it was a totally a pointless exercise. You couldn't see him, he was smoking and there was a random dog in the shot.

I'd heard all the warnings, but everyone told me Colin Farrell was a bad boy and he ended up asking me to go for a night out with him and telling me we could be bad boys together. This did not look like it was heading for a happy ending, though. More like a total massive waste of time.

It was up there with one of the weirdest situations I'd been in, just behind Slash. I got to the end of the pointless interview and all my enthusiasm had disappeared a long time ago. But, just like when I met Steve Coogan, I stayed polite to the end, said 'Thanks for your time,' gave the dog a pat and off I went – 'See ya later.' I still couldn't see him clearly because of all the smoke.

One of his people asked me on the way out: 'Can you use that?' 'What do you reckon?' I thought. But never mind, I was on my bike.

I'd almost reached the hotel exit when I heard a woman chasing after me, shouting 'Tubes, Tubes, Tubes!' I stopped and turned around. 'Mickey Rourke would like you to go back to the room,' she said.

I went back up and he was sat there. Hadn't moved an inch. 'I'm sorry,' he said. 'Let's do the question again and I won't smoke. The dog had also gone. I have never found out to this day why he asked me back. I didn't really want to ask. So I did it and it turned out really nicely. I don't know what I did or what people said to earn me a second chance, but he said: 'Thanks for that, I really enjoyed it, hope you enjoyed it too.'

Can't say I did the first one, but the second one was completely different.

The whole episode will definitely go down as one of the weirdest interviews I've done. Mainly because it wasn't even part of the act and his people and the organisers were just letting him do it, even though they must have known that wasn't going to help them plug the film. Then for me to make my excuses and leave and get almost out of the hotel, only to be asked back. He certainly lived up to the bad boy reputation.

Thankfully the interview with John Cena, a real wrestler, made for better TV. He flipped the whole thing on its head by impressing me with his rapping ability and showing me how it's really done:

> Tubes: Hi John, I'm Tubes from *Soccer AM*. I've got One Question and One Question Only.
> John Cena: Right, what's your question?
> T: I'm hitting you with the Tubesy flow, oh my gosh it's the people's elbow [mouth noise], you can't see me!

His response blew me away as he delivered an off-the-cuff freestyle that put me right in my place.

> JC: Ahem. Not much of a question, stop ya stressing, listen to a real freestyler, I'll teach ya a lesson, yeah that's right, you know Tott'nham got 'em, it's in the street, Arsenal straight beat, tonight is the big match, I'm gonna take it back to the sw-sw-swi-swatch, I do your own gimmick, that's why I'm up in it, with the rewind, perfect T-I-M-E, time, check the shirt, HLR, you can't see me I'm like a fast car, but not Tracy Chapman, you got man, that's OK, I sing like Scatman, I keep it on the beat, with the verses, keep my sh** clean, no curses, bleep out my own rhymes, in my own time, I'm like a ding-ding, you hear my own chime, the champ is here, we right in the ring, John Cena, I'm doing my thing, check out the Royal Rumble and Wrestlemania, yeah that's right kid, my freestyle

is saving ya, you got two bars, I got 40 plus,
there ain't nothing better than us.

I tried to pretend I wasn't fazed, just brushed off his effort as if I could do it in my sleep and carried on. But the truth was he was incredible. They didn't even prep him. He just came out with it on the spot. All I could do was admit: 'I've just been totally beaten here.'

I didn't even remember what my four lines were by the time he finished his 40. I just had to take it on the chin. John Cena has absolutely ruined me. Absolutely ruined me.

I was determined to come back with something special the next week, to try and show the lessons John Cena had taught me had been learned. Then reality hit me during the week as I tried to plot my comeback – I'm actually not very good.

It was a bit of a savage beating against John Cena but at least I didn't end up in hospital. One of the greatest wrestlers of all time nearly made sure that I did though – Hulk Hogan. It was not the reward I was expecting for making a huge effort for one of the sport's absolute legends.

The Hulk Hogan interview was thrust on me just the day before. He was actually appearing on Sky News when someone suggested to him he should do something for *Soccer AM*. He was fine about it and it was a plug for him.

I was late for work the next day but still on time to meet Hulk Hogan at 10.30am. Well, I thought I was. Because I then got a call at 9.45 a.m. to say 'Hulk Hogan is waiting for you.'

All I had time for was a quick raid of the props cupboard to find a yellow T-shirt, red banana and cut a slit in the T-shirt so I could actually rip it during my act. I was quite proud of the Hulk Hogan costume I managed to rustle up, all in about 28 seconds.

Not sure he was, though. Or maybe it was my rapping that upset him:

> Tubes: Hi Hulk, I'm Tubes from *Soccer AM*, I've got One Question and One Question Only. You're a top man, you're Mr Hogan, you're up there like Terry Wogan, ooooohhhhh, I'm a real Surrey man, fight for your life for the Cobham man [cheek wobble], oooh Hulk these lyrics are really killing me.
> Hulk Hogan: STRAIGHTEN UP!

His response caught me totally off guard as he launched at me and locked me in a choke hold. This definitely was not in the script. He took the wind right out of me and I ended up slumped into the sofa we were standing next to.

He was hurting me so much. I was in agony. I thought I was going to pass out and was definitely seeing stars. I couldn't really breathe either. He was choking the life out of me. I was trying to act and say something silly but I just couldn't get the words out. I could just about make out him saying 'Another one down,' then it all went a little hazy for a few seconds.

I tried to act calm when I staggered back to my feet and ask him a question. But you can hear when you watch it back that I was struggling to get the words out.

There was no acting here. I thought he twisted something in my neck and did me some real damage.

Hulk Hogan is an absolute brute. He must be one of the biggest men I have ever seen. He's got to be about 60 years old as well, and has the biggest hands I've ever seen, bigger than any goalkeeper's.

Just before it was time to go, he grabbed my tiny girl's hands with one of his slabs and I spotted an opportunity to get him back in my own little way. As we shook I started tickling the palm of his hand with one of my fingers. 'Quit tickling the palm of my hand with your finger,' he said menacingly. I didn't fancy being strangled again. So I stopped. 'Thank you,' and off he went.

Meanwhile, by 11 o'clock I was heading back to my desk having got into work and just been strangled by Hulk Hogan. Just another average day at Sky Towers.

PS: Hulk Hogan is a proper big name. But walking through the corridors with him, he was nice as he could be. Everybody was stunned to see him just casually walking by, and once they picked their jaws off the ground they all wanted a piece of him. Yet he had no problem stopping and speaking to everybody. He was nice to everyone. It was refreshing to see.

CHAPTER 14

BOXING HELL!

The thing about Hulk Hogan almost putting me in hospital was it was just a bit of a muck-about that went wrong. He was in character – and I paid the price.

When boxer Chris Eubank appeared on *Soccer AM* we genuinely couldn't tell if he was acting or not.

The first boxer I had met on the show was Nigel Benn. He was one seriously cool guy. Well spoken, well mannered and generally left a good impression in terms of what boxers were like.

It's quite well known Chris Eubank is a bit eccentric. That's a good way to describe him. You just have to look at the way he boxed, his clothes and dress sense (he does wear some proper rascal gear), his mannerisms, or the big truck that he drives. Well, he didn't leave any of that stuff at home when he came to *Soccer AM*.

He drove down in a massive blue truck for starters and then swaggered into the studio with a cane. And that was just the start of it. The whole interview was puzzling. I couldn't work him out and neither could anybody else.

I went on to interview an incredibly clever boxer in Wladimir Klitschko. Now I look back, Chris Eubank didn't show the same depth, to my mind. Halfway through the show, he just ended the interview and walked off, got back in his big truck and drove off into the distance, with no explanation. Guests usually stay until the end so it's probably no surprise to hear we were caught out. All he said was: 'I'm going, I'm going now.'

As you can imagine, it was all pretty awkward trying to explain why our guest count had just dropped, when we didn't actually have an explanation. He left during the ad break. He was on the sofa before we cut to adverts and gone when we were back on air. It was a bit awkward for Tim to explain, but not as awkward as it could have been.

Watching it back, it is almost like he is trying to drop hints that he wants to go. He's hardly sitting on the sofa or looking interested in what the other guests were saying.

The guys from *The Mighty Boosh* were on the show at the same time. Obviously, they like a laugh, and the slightly off-the-wall guy who had been sitting next to them gave them a fair bit of ammo. With him now gone, they thought the coast was clear and it was safe to crack a few jokes at his expense. They claimed he did a runner because he was scared of them.

What they didn't know was Chris Eubank hadn't quite left the building. And before they even had a chance to finish laughing, out of nowhere, he came sprinting back into the studio and charged at Noel Fielding. It was a total mismatch. A former world boxing champion versus a comedian who, as much as I love him, isn't the hardest-looking man around town.

We actually thought Chris Eubank was seriously trying to fight him. Genuinely thought that, especially the way he came running back onto the set with a look of real intent.

I was standing backstage making some tea after he'd left. Then, out the corner of my eye, I just saw him come flying down the corridor. He must have seen the rest of the guests carry on talking about him while he sat in the green room backstage, the waiting room where we keep our guests.

When he got back into the studio and jumped on Noel Fielding on the sofa, there were a few seconds where I thought 'He is actually going to knock him out'. Everyone's hearts were in their mouths for a brief moment as we feared for Noel. The crew didn't know whether to jump in and rescue him or not.

When we realised Chris Eubank was actually just play-fighting it was like the whole studio let out a group sigh of relief. Phew, that was close.

Tim and Helen thought it was hilarious, and Tim even fell off the sofa he was laughing so much. Noel Fielding didn't find it quite as funny. He absolutely wet himself. He tried to laugh it off but you could tell he was genuinely scared, especially as Chris Eubank flew back into view while he was looking away:

Noel Fielding: God, that was a frightening sight!

Tim Lovejoy: Do you need some tissues or something?

NF: I actually wet my trousers. It was so late that I saw it and my fringe was in the way.

TL: Otherwise you'd have done him yeah?

NF: What the cameras didn't pick up was as he got in close I pinched him.

TL: [Still in tears, laughing] That scared me, that was brilliant.

NF: Ahhh I can't breathe!

After seeing Eubank do that I thought you should be wary of all boxers, but Wladimir Klitschko showed me this wasn't true when we met a few weeks before his fight against David Haye.

He was brilliant. Such a top bloke. I actually interviewed him before that as well, a sit-down one before he was supposed to fight Dereck Chisora. (He is a doughnut by the way – he actually thought he had a chance of beating Big Wlad… Dream on!) Wladimir Klitschko was really interesting and one of the cleverest people I've met.

You think as a boxer, someone whose life is all about being walloped around the head, that they aren't exactly going to be Mr Brainy. But his philosophy on boxing and life was unbelievable. He said he liked being a boxer because it meant he could see the world, and if he wasn't a boxer he'd be an air steward.

Just to try and get a reaction I said: 'An air stewardess?' But he was so switched on and shot me down: 'No, an air steward.' He wanted to travel and that was the reason he loved boxing.

He said his and his brother Vitali's domination of the heavyweight division was all down to the way they'd been brought up. They never really had a fight when they were younger, but they trained relentlessly.

He said boxing is all in your head and not about how hard you can punch someone. You see everyone trash-talking before fights, but Wladimir Klitschko is not particularly interested in all that. When you are expecting boxers to start scrapping at the weigh-in stare-off, he is just like he was in the interview, cool, calm and collected. Just like he was when I put him on the spot about David Haye, who he wasn't that fond of at the time, but he managed to swerve the question nicely:

Tubes: You're a top man and I love you. You're one of my favourite boxers. What I want to know is what do you like best about David Haye?
Wladimir Klitschko: What do I like best of David Haye?
T: Yeah.
WK: [20 seconds' silence] Did you get the answer? I just said it.
T: You said nothing.
WK: You missed it? You missed it?
T: You must like something about him?
WK: I just said it.
T: Okay, what don't you like about David Haye then?

WK: Don't like? [More silence]

T: His hair?

WK: I just said it. You didn't hear me?

T: No. I have got talcum powder in me ears.

WK: It was pretty loud. If you look into my eyes [Tubes stares in] you can read a lot. The eyes are the mirror of the soul. They can give you answers and ask you questions. Did you get my answer?

T: Yes I did.

WK: Clear as the day.

T: Great answer. Thanks a lot.

WK: Thank you for asking.

T: Cheers. No worries.

Wladimir Klitschko compared boxing to art and said the whole sport was in your head if you believed you would win. To me if someone punches you square in the face that's it, game over (take Fenners' right hook on Tim for example!). But if that is how he sees boxing there must be something in it, because he's not bad, is he?

I thought before I interviewed him that he'd just be an absolute brute who was big and loud like most boxers and that's about it. But I was astonished at how clever and thoughtful he was.

Amir Khan was another top bloke, but for different reasons – he gave Dev, one of the guys I work with, a right good going over. And to be fair, he deserved it.

Dev was doing some research on Amir Khan in the week leading up to him being on the show and found a stat he reckoned was rubbish. It said Amir Khan had such fast hands he could lay five punches in just one second. Dev was having none of it and was happily telling everyone in the office: 'That's impossible and I would quite happily tell that to his face.'

What a silly, silly boy. He probably should have guessed what was going to happen next. Saturday comes around and I come out to do my One Question and One Question Only. It is only going to be for one man and about one thing:

> Tubes: Hi Amir, I'm Tubes from *Soccer AM*, I've got One Question and One Question Only. You're a top man, you're not a prance, in my spare time I'm a sexy dancer, I'm a sexy dancer, I'm a sexy dancer! You are a top bloke and I love you. You claim that you can do five punches in a second.
> Amir Khan: Yep. I can.
> T: My mate Dev says you're not very hard, you can't do it and it wouldn't hurt him even if you could.
> [Out walked a padded-up Dev.]
> T: So take it away my friend.

Up he got off the sofa, with his tailored blazer still on and unleashed fury on poor Dev's stomach. It was pretty impressive. He absolutely smashed him out the ball park. I wouldn't like to get into a fight with Amir Khan, based on that display, or any boxer for that matter. It was frightening. He would seriously injure most people. At least break my neck if he punched me in the face. Dev somehow stayed up, so wind-up merchant Helen got involved.

> H: Dev said you can't get much power behind
> five punches.
> T: He said you aren't very hard.
> H: And he said you're a weed.

Amir Khan went again and this time Dev fell to the floor in agony. We had to drag him off because he couldn't get back up again. He probably felt how I did after Hulk Hogan's choke hold... and a bit worse. Dev tried to claim it didn't hurt but he said it while he struggled to get his words out and could hardly breathe. The one thing he did manage to spit out was: 'Blooming hell, he is so quick.'

Another boxer we had on the show was memorable: Audley Harrison. He was a guest not long after he won the Olympics, which was great for our country and all that. Well done.

There was an excited buzz among the crew about getting him on so soon after winning his gold medal. That soon disappeared when we eventually showed up with the biggest entourage of 'people'. I've never seen one like it.

We've had big names on the show. The likes of Noel Gallagher and all that who don't bring anyone and just roll up on their own. Audley Harrison brought about seven or eight heavies with him. All massive geezers that surrounded him every step he took. It seemed like they were his mates.

A lot of us couldn't believe Audley Harrison needed heavies at all, let alone that many, especially when he was coming to a fun, morning show like *Soccer AM*, and he has such a powerful physique.

'I want fried breakfasts for everyone. They all want orange juice.' He said this to my brother Big Ange, who was just 16 at the time and on work experience on the show.

Audley was well all right on subsequent visits to the show, so fair play. Perhaps winning the gold medal (don't get me wrong, it's a massive achievement) had affected him. On camera he was fine. Charming. But that's what always happens. Behind the camera he was full of himself.

Nancy Dell'Olio, the former England manager Sven Goran Eriksson's girlfriend for a while, turned up to the show armed with a list of requests, like many celebs. Hers were about what we should and should not talk to her about.

The year after when she came back on, nobody really cared about her. She'd split up with Sven and dropped off everybody's radar. We had her on the last show of the season and, a little bit to get back at her, we put her outside cooking sausages for everyone, which was quite funny. 'Come on Nancy, cook those sausages for us!' Ha-ha. Hopefully she learned her lesson.

By the time Audley Harrison came back on the show five or six years later he had changed and was a really nice bloke then – and to this day he still is. Maybe winning the Olympics just got to him a little bit.

When he arranged his fight with David Haye in 2010 they were supposed to come on the show together. I thought it was a mistake because as they were building up to the fight there was a real hatred between them. Thankfully David

Haye didn't show up; nobody knew why. When we finally caught up with him, he said: 'I didn't know I was supposed to come on.'

Looking back on it his not coming on was probably for the best. Those two sitting next to each other just a week before the fight after they'd spent all the build-up slagging each other off, could have been disastrous. Another Chris Eubank moment for us while we're watching through our fingers, scared about what's going to happen. Actually, it would've probably been even worse than Chris Eubank. Harrison v. Haye would be a more hardcore fight than Eubank v. Noel Fielding!

I know exactly what I would have been like if they both showed up – I've never had a fight in my life so I'm not sticking around for this! I'm a tin-pot rapper, get me out of here!

TUBES EXTRA

FAVOURITE *SOCCER AM* MOMENTS

Tim Lovejoy getting punched straight in the face by accident (I think!) by Fenners! Fenners was dressed as an Aussie Rules player at the time, which it made it all the more funny. David Haye would have been proud of that right-hander!

Pearl diving. My goodness the old girl can dive, I've watched it about 100 times and it still creases me up, especially when she pulls out the somersault, Tom Daley take note!

My colleague (who will remain nameless) booking Sean Williamson (Barry from *EastEnders*) when he was convinced he'd booked the footballer Shaun Goater! The best line I've ever heard in the *Soccer AM* office: 'Tubes this is mad mate, Shaun Goater is doing pantomime these days. How weird is that, and he's also landed himself a part in Ricky Gervais's *Extras*!' I cried with laughter for days.

Playing the first game at the new Wembley. I couldn't believe what was happening, what an awesome experience. I played all right, too!

Serge from Kasabian's unreal strike at the end game; that will never be beaten. He's refused to have a kick since and to be honest I don't blame him – finish your football career at the top I say!

Frank McAvennie firing a ball straight into Fenners' massive conk. To be fair it's quite a big target ha-ha. From then on the car park was known as 'The Frank McAvennie car park'.

Kammy doing a pre-match tour of Portsmouth. Without warning he burst into the manager's office and there was the legend that is Harry Redknapp with Jim Smith sitting reading the *Racing Post*!

Helen showing off a really impressive model of Stamford Bridge (apparently it took months to put together) and dropping it, smashing it into thousands of pieces. Of course I was also heartbroken, as I wanted to take it home!

FAVOURITE *SOCCER AM* MOMENTS

Soccer AM playing a massive part in getting the World Cup star to put on the England shirt.

CHAPTER 15

COME ON ENGLAND!

Penalties and winning major tournaments. Two things England have not proved to be very good at during my lifetime.

But banter? Now that's a different story. If banter won you trophies we wouldn't still be talking about the good old days of 1966. No, no, no. England would be in the position Spain are right now. We would have a new squad of heroes, be the best team on the planet and going to walk the World Cup in Brazil next year. Because our boys have got buckets of banter and there is something about *Soccer AM* that seems to bring it out of all of them.

I have probably met most of the current team now and England's no.1 Joe Hart is probably one of the nicest people I've met in football. Considering goalkeepers are supposed to be mad he is a clever bloke. Really clever. As for his banter – well it's up there with some of the best I've heard.

He didn't pay me to say that. I am just being fair to him after he once called me the funniest man in football (probably so I left him alone sharpish – seriously, who wants to see a fat lad do a truffle shuffle in front of you?) Him, Micah Richards and Leighton Baines were in stitches after I entertained them with a rap and my truffle shuffle dance at a red-carpet England function once.

Seriously, though, the clip of Joe Hart doing his pencil dance shows he deserves the praise. That video is a *Soccer AM* favourite. At the time it got leaked it must have been one of the most viewed videos in the world.

If somehow you haven't seen the clip of Joe Hart in action during a trip with England Under-21s, firstly you have to. Secondly, in the clip he walks into the room and points to all his imaginary fans before starting to wave his hands around in all directions like an absolute nutcase when the music starts. Then he puts his hands by his side and starts leaping around like an absolute nutcase.

When I found out I was going to meet him I just had to ask how the hell he came up with it. The dance, he said, was made up on a night out when he was in a club and charged up – on Red Bull, he promised me. One of his mates started doing the dance, but there were only three or four people in the club so nobody really got to see it. So he showed his roommate Nedum Onuoha (who he also played with at Manchester City at the time) the dance... and then the whole world got to see it.

Nedum Onuoha filmed it and asked if he could put the

clip up on a few websites. Joe Hart said yes, maybe not realising that one of the websites was YouTube. You know, the one that pretty much every person in the whole world goes on to watch videos. It is still one of the best clips I have seen of a footballer getting up to silly antics in their own time. Joe Hart properly goes for it in his demonstration of the dance for Nedum Onuoha.

As a tribute to Joe Hart, I decided to copy his dance in the *Soccer AM* dance-off earlier this year. Thanks to him I came second. He watched it as well and told me, 'I was proud of you mate, but you should have put a bit more effort into it.' Obviously that is a bit easy for him to say as a super-fit professional athlete. I'm not. I was blowing after about 10 seconds and had other moves to do. Plus my armpits were starting to smell! Even a little half-hearted I thought I'd done enough to win, though. But Rocket pipped me to the title because he practiced... like he does every year.

The other thing I really wanted to speak to Joe Hart about was life as a goalkeeper. Imagine playing in goal and having hordes of away fans behind you – what must that be like? And when you play for one of the big clubs like Manchester City it can be quite lonely at times, just him all on his own in his penalty area.

I was intrigued and he gave me a bit of an insight. He told me about some of the shocking abuse, and there was one occasion that really stood out. He was getting battered by someone all through the game who was telling him he was rubbish and claiming she could do better than him. Then, when he turned around expecting to see maybe a mouthy teenager it was actually an old woman who looked comfortably in her 70s, who had probably never played football before in her life, but who didn't rate him and felt the need to tell him for 90 minutes.

Because of the type of laid-back character he is, Joe Hart said things like that were brilliant and help make football. He was so down to earth and his attitude was: 'Yeah I get abused, but how lucky am I to be doing what I do?'

It was also refreshing to see and hear from England's no.1 that he still can't believe how well he has done. He is another person I would love to go on a night out with and have a dance-off with, to learn from the best.

When it comes to being humble, there can't be too many professional footballers like this more than Tottenham defender Kyle Walker. During our chat it seemed to hit him how well he has done in his career. I said to him: 'Your mum and dad must be so proud.'

'It's funny you say that,' he said. 'Me and my girlfriend were sitting watching *X-Factor* the other day watching this kid do really well and I said a little comment about how well they'd done. My girlfriend turned to me and said, 'well, that's what your mum and dad must think of you,' and that's when it hit home that hopefully I've made my family proud.'

I bet they are well proud of him. It was nice to hear a modern day footballer be so down to earth and concerned about such a thing, when they could be really arrogant if they wanted to be.

He had no problem mucking around a bit too. At the start of the interview we did a bit of acting, which was hilarious. We got him to pretend to be on the phone to his girlfriend and slating me by saying: 'Yeah I'm just waiting around to meet this doughnut called Tubes.' Then all of a sudden I walk into the shot and he switches, hangs up the phone and greets me like I'm a long lost friend. He was nervous about doing it, but he pulled it off like a natural. Nailed it first time, Oscar-winning performance. He also taught me the secret handshake that he does with teammate Jake Livermore.

But one of the funniest parts of the interview was his answer to what is the difference between London to Sheffield apart from the accent. His answer was instant: 'The traffic.' And he followed it up with a hilarious quote, one of the best I've heard. 'The traffic down here, a 5-minute journey can take you 15 to 20 minutes. Up in Sheffield, you can get somewhere that's supposed to take you five minutes in four minutes.' Classic.

Alex Oxlade-Chamberlain was just as impressive, but for different reasons. When I spoke to The Ox, as I will call him, the thing that shocked me was that he was only 18, at the time. He speaks so well and I reckon he's got a future in TV presenting. He's already done a bit for Arsenal's official website with Ox TV.

Straight away we got on really well. Like Joe Hart he also got caught on camera doing something that he needed to be pulled up on. Not long after he joined Arsenal there was a clip that appeared on the internet of The Ox singing Nikki Minaj while driving. I asked him to prove it was no fluke by drop some bars again, and to be fair to him he's got a good voice and some good rhythm.

The second time I met him he revealed he knew all the

words to the *Fresh Prince of Bel Air* theme tune, and you could tell he loved proving it. He said: 'We've got to work together in the future and do stuff for Ox TV, watch this space, watch this space.' So that's another future project for me!

The Ox's Arsenal teammate Theo Walcott revealed that he is often genuinely mistaken for Lewis Hamilton. I thought he was kidding. They look a little bit similar but you would think people would be able to tell the difference. But, no, he said people really do think he is the F1 driver. People have even approached him in the streets and said: 'Well done Lewis, great race the other day.' He is too polite to say anything and just lets them think he is Lewis Hamilton. Because of all the F1 talk, we ended up doing car impressions – as you do –and making the noises of F1 cars whizzing around the track like kids!

He was really open too. For a laugh I said: 'You're rapid, aren't you?' He said: 'Yeah I'm quick, quick.' 'If you weren't quick,' I said, 'would you be any good at football?' Because he is so relaxed he just shrugged his shoulders and said: 'Nah, nah, I wouldn't be a professional footballer.'

This was obviously just a light-hearted conversation, but one paper picked up on it and ran a story the next day along the lines of 'Theo Walcott says if he wasn't quick he wouldn't be a footballer'. It was a shame because if you watch the interview you can see he is just having a laugh. He got into the idea of the show because he watches it. It's nice to walk in and hear him say: 'Ah good interview the other week.'

I interviewed Peter Crouch on the same day as Theo

Walcott at Wembley and we hardly spent any time talking about football. The interview was not too long after Peter Crouch became a father. He showed me how his nappy-making skills were getting on, and I tell you what, he's got unbelievable nappy tekkers.

I was gutted it didn't make the final cut, because it was really good to see a player doing a really normal thing. He actually brought it up by saying how much he loved being a dad, it's amazing and then we started talking about nappies. It was strange walking around Wembley talking to one of England's main strikers at the time but the topic of conversation was baby poo.

It didn't surprise me that Peter Crouch was a laid back guy, who didn't mind joking around. I think that was obvious when he said he would be a virgin if he wasn't a professional footballer. And also when he introduced the world to his robot dance. I tried to get him to do the robot but he was having none of it. 'It's been done now. I've done the robot,' he said. 'If I score a screamer I might bring it back.' But since then he hasn't scored a screamer so we're still waiting!

I told him: 'I've made a new dance – the pencil dance,' and tried to get him to start a craze like the robot, which everyone was doing before the World Cup in 2006. It was a bit like Joe Hart's but all straight. No bending at the hip and knees. Just bobbing up and down with your hands over your head, palms together. Ages ago he promised me he would do it next time he scored but he still hasn't so I'm still waiting Crouchie.

On a more serious note, Peter Crouch was also quite open

about his relationship with Fabio Capello and said the former England manager never really gave him the time of day. He felt there was no point lying about it and said that he didn't really like him, and he felt the feeling was mutual. It was quite good to get out of him at the time.

I have always thought Fabio Capello looked like Postman Pat so to try and cheer Peter Crouch up I mentioned it to him. I asked Theo Walcott what he thought about the comparison and I reckon he wanted to agree, but obviously he couldn't, so he just laughed.

The Jermain Defoe interview was a random one, especially the way it came about. He invited me round to his house, which was quite nice. I got hold of him on Twitter and asked if I could interview him and he replied pretty quickly: 'Yeah come round on Monday, just speak to Jade Ruben, one of my representatives (who is lovely by the way). So I went around to his house and sat on his sofa and we had a chat. There was just no hassle to it at all, which was a surprise, considering he is one of England's top strikers.

I have heard some people say he's got an attitude, but he hasn't at all. In fact he is completely the opposite. He also does a hell of a lot of charity work. Actually, if his film choices are anything to go by he's a bit of a softie – he said he loved watching romantic films, especially that film *The Notebook*.

He said he wanted to start a boyband at Spurs and also revealed that his middle name is Colin. I am sure some people might have known that, but he decided to tell the whole world just to make sure. I was killing him for that and he wasn't happy. 'Mum, mum, why would you do that to me?' he said into the camera. 'Jermain Colin Defoe? I can't have that.'

He was another top bloke. So down to earth. Actually, they all were. And it made me feel for them a bit, knowing how they get slated so much at times when they are just normal guys.

We always go into tournaments thinking, 'we should be winning this,' and I've never been able to work out why we never really seem to do as well as we should, or believe we should.

If you look at the players we've got and had while I have been alive they've always been top footballers. Frank Lampard, Steven Gerrard, Wayne Rooney – all great players. They might not have won anything for England, but with the likes of the Ox, Theo Walcott, Tom Cleverley, Phil Jones and Joe Hart – possibly the best keeper in the world, by the way – the future looks good, if you ask me.

And if we can start getting extra goals for our banter, that would be even better.

CHAPTER 16

UNDERWEAR BANDITS

As well as being a tin-pot rapper, the part of my job I absolutely buzz off is getting the opportunity to sit down with the Premier League's finest, and have a chat about everything... from football to Peter Crouch changing nappies. I love football, and to be honest my life would be very boring without it (and that's probably the same for the majority of people reading this book).

So when I was given the chance about four seasons ago by my boss at Sky, Rob Wakeling, to do a sit down interview with Darren Bent I jumped at the chance. Again I was a bit nervous, because this was new to me. It wasn't just a gangster rap and a random one question. I didn't want to just ask about football. You know, the usual stuff: 'Big game coming up at the weekend, isn't it?' etc. I wanted to find out more about the player himself. His hobbies and interests outside of the game, as well as keeping the beautiful game within the conversation.

So with Darren Bent I asked questions about him growing up playing football, a little bit about the banter at Sunderland, where he was playing at the time, and him going trick or treating. I just like to find stuff out that people may not have known, things that are a little bit different.

And it's a real buzz when you leave an interview with something that's never been 'out there'. If it's funny too that is perfect for *Soccer AM*, as that's what we're all about. It helps massively if the player wants to do something, like when Jim Carrey wanted to learn all the Chelsea songs.

Gareth Bale was similar. On the day I met him he was more than happy to sit down for *Soccer AM*, I guess because he knew it would be a laugh and a joke. Sometimes when I am doing the pre-interview research I come across something that I have never seen mentioned before. That was the case with Gareth Bale. He took a look a little while to warm up, but once he got going there was no stopping him. A bit like when he's bombing up and down the pitch.

I tried getting him to reveal all about the heart celebration that he does after all the millions of goals he has scored. He wouldn't tell. Not a word. I bugged him and bugged him but he just wouldn't say. All he did say was that you would find out soon, so I guess it is a case of watch this space.

I couldn't have got Gareth Bale at a better time. It was the morning after he won the PFA Player of the Year and Young Player of the Year awards. Understandably he was buzzing.

So I said to him: 'Gareth, a few seasons ago you couldn't

get a game at Spurs and now you're one of the world's best players. What's happened?'

'I've got better,' he said. Thanks Gareth, I thought, great insight!

Seriously, though, that is how down to earth he is. Just such a cool, normal guy who at the same time happens to be one of the best players in the world. I wanted to laugh at his answer, big time, but I had to hold it in and just push him a bit by asking how he had actually got better and what sort of things he had been doing to make him so good. In terms of quotes I have got, it's up there with Kyle Walker's about the five-minute journey that somehow takes four minutes.

But Gareth Bale saved the best for last – his story about being an underwear bandit with Theo Walcott when they were in the academy at Southampton.

He and Theo Walcott were really good friends and used to live in a massive house for all the academy kids in Southampton when they were coming through the ranks. For some reason, when they used to get bored they would grab their pillows, put underwear on their heads and go around the academy building and batter all the other unsuspecting kids with pillows.

One of the first questions that sprang to mind was: 'Why on earth put underwear on your heads?' And he promised they were clean. Promised. That is definitely one of the most bizarre things I've ever been told by a footballer.

The secret that Liverpool legend Jamie Carragher told me was a great one – but could quite easily have got me the sack.

I knew he was joining Sky after retiring at the end of last season, but not many other people in the footballing and media world did. I said: 'Can I ask you about it?' 'Yeah,' he said.

He ended up saying something along the lines of: 'Yeah it will be cool, I can't wait, I'm really looking forward to it, but you're the main man Tubes.' To which I replied swiftly: 'No Jamie, you're the main man!'

'We'll go for pints when we're at work and stuff. It'll be great,' he added.

It was great stuff so I put together the package with Jamie Carragher talking about his next move after retirement in it. I was buzzing about it. Everyone was trying to second-guess what his next move was going to be – fans, the media, even other TV channels – and we had the answer along with him talking about it.

Something was nagging away at me, though, and telling me to check whether anyone was supposed to know. I sensed I could get in a lot of trouble for this if I didn't so I checked with the top boss at Sky and he emailed me back: 'Sorry Tubes, that hasn't been released yet, so *make sure* that doesn't go out.'

I was *that* close to putting it out... but it turned out to be a very lucky escape. If I hadn't checked with the top boss, I would've let the cat out of the bag and Jamie Carragher's big 'next move' announcement could have been ruined long before it was supposed to be made public. If it had gone out the least I would've got was an almighty hairdryer treatment from the big boss.

It's especially good when players let slip things that the

fans can't see or won't have seen. I think it is great to get an insight into their lives and the things they see that we usually can't.

For example, I would've loved to have seen what Bobby Zamora said he saw when he played for Fulham under Roy Hodgson. When I asked Bobby, who is now at QPR, what was the funniest thing he had ever seen in a changing room, straight away the answer came to him: Roy Hodgson walking around with a ghetto blaster on his shoulder dancing around, with 'Land Down Under' by Men at Work blaring out of the speakers.

You can't imagine the England manager or even a character like Roy Hodgson letting their hair down, let alone going that far. Bobby Zamora said it was one of the most surreal things he has ever seen – and let me repeat for those still in shock: Roy Hodgson giving it large to 'Land Down Under'.

Initially, Bobby Zamora said he was so shocked he didn't know what to do. But once he realised what he was seeing was really happening he knew the gaffer with his guard down was a special moment that needed to be shared with his teammates. 'Duffer, Duffer, Duffer, come look at this,' he screamed at Damien Duff. And then in the corner Roy Hodgson is still in his own world dancing around. Obviously they were all in stitches. Roy Hodgson is clearly a real character and funny man, not at all what you see on TV.

Arsene Wenger is another manager who is not all that he seems, according to Arsenal midfielder Aaron Ramsey. He reckons his boss has got plenty of banter and loves winding the players up, especially when they hit a bad shot in training and he shouts 'Ooohhh-la-laaa!'

Aaron Ramsey said everyone thinks he is miserable – and you do always see the tantrums, but behind closed doors he's a very funny man and has people in stitches. I couldn't believe it when he said Arsene Wenger had a bit of banter. I can't imagine it. Whenever you see him he never seems to look that happy, and is quite often having a go at the officials. So to hear someone talking about him mucking around really surprised me.

So did James Milner – twice. Firstly with his confession that he's never had a beer in his life. Footballers have got loads of money and opportunities to go to places all over the world, especially in the summer – they're here, there and everywhere, having a good time. But James Milner never has. Certainly not under the influence of alcohol anyway. But he argues that's why he's done well in his career and is super fit.

Then we got on to food. We were talking about pre-match meals and he was saying nowadays cereal is a bit more common. I asked him what he had and he said: 'Gone are the days of having steak and things like that, because it could end up with someone having an accident.'

'Have you ever seen that?' I said. 'Maybe?' he said. 'Come on. What's the story? 'Nah, nah, nah,' he said, before finally spilling the beans – sort of.

He wouldn't reveal who the player was, but did say: 'I was at Newcastle and we were playing Blackburn, I think. I won't tell you what season it was, but someone had to run off really sharpish because they needed a number two. But I won't mention any names.'

That mystery remains unsolved. I might have to try and get him back on to finish off the story.

TUBES EXTRA

SOME THINGS YOU MAY OR MAY NOT KNOW

West Brom's striker Shane Long is top class on the guitar and his party piece is playing and singing 'No Woman, No Cry' by Bob Marley. Top bloke, top footballer and top musician.

Arsenal midfielder Mikel Arteta could have been a professional tennis player, and he also wore a pair of football boots signed by myself against Villa. Couldn't quite believe it!

I have webbed toes on both feet... Yes, freak. I should have been a good swimmer, but I'm not.

TUBESOLOGY

Tottenham striker Jermain Defoe wants to start up a boy band up with Jermaine Jenas, Sandro and another teammate. And did I mention his middle name is Colin?

Carlton Cole always dreamt of being Superman when he was younger. To make his dream come true, even if it was just for a few seconds, when we told the story we superimposed his head onto Superman's body. Apparently he got battered by his teammates for letting that slip. If he wasn't a footballer now he would like to be a fireman.

Swansea defender Ashley Williams learnt Spanish for two reasons. First, so he could communicate with all his teammates more easily – clever boy! But the best reason is so that most of the opposition players don't have a clue what they're talking about when they start talking tactics. Ashley also said Swansea is such a close-knit community he often has fans come around to his house and knock on his front door and ask him to sign things. Can you imagine that happening to a Man United or Chelsea player in one of their plush mansions?

My *Soccer AM* colleague Rocket is called Rocket because he was born with a pointy head.

The Australian actor Hugh Jackman, who is most famous for playing Wolverine in the *X-Men* films, is a Norwich fan. Random.

Southampton legend Matt Le Tissier is addicted to cold (yes cold) cheese and tomato sauce sandwiches... Rascal sandwich.

Wolves defender Roger Johnson loves American R&B group Boyz II Men and once sung one of their songs in an interview for *Soccer AM* to prove it. He's a good singer, to be fair. He is also good at doing impressions of a wolf. His howling is impressive.

Liverpool legend Robbie Fowler – Haaa-lle-lu-jah! – is really good mates with the singer Chris de Burgh. Chris and his family (including his dog) send Robbie Fowler – Haaa-lle-lu-jah! –– Christmas cards. Chris made the dog stand in ink and then walk across the card. Also Robbie Fowler – Haaa-lle-lu-jah! – has got Chris's song 'Lady in Red' down to a T.

When asked to pick five items to make his perfect fry-up, Manchester United God Ryan Giggs said sausage, egg, beans, bacon and toast... What would yours be?

I was an extra in the film *Goal 3*... fat face, silly hair and Bertie Budget film.

CHAPTER 17

EVERYONE LIKES A HUG, DON'T THEY?

It's not only some of the things footballers have said that have been memorable, but also some of the things they have done during interviews too.

Unfortunately, though, it often involves some kind of pain or suffering for me. Like when I met the former Fulham goalkeeper Mark Schwarzer last season. (He would run Hulk Hogan close in a Royal Rumble).

Every time I interview a Fulham player I always text their midfielder Steve Sidwell asking for inside information – sorry for outing you if you're reading this Steve. I get on quite well with him and want to know if he has got any dirt on the teammate I am about to interview.

When I asked before meeting Mark Schwarzer he replied: 'Mate, I'm not giving you anything on Mark Schwarzer because that guy is double-hard and he has this punishment he gives people called the bear hug.'

Without even realising, Steve Sidwell had given me something worth looking into – Mark Schwarzer's bear hug. 'He's never got me with it,' Steve said 'because I never say anything bad to him. But the guys who have received the bear hug, *know* about the bear hug.' That was all the invitation I needed. I knew I had to ask for one.

The interview started off with a really good chat about Fulham and Australia, or the Socceroos. It was interesting that he said the old Leeds and Middlesbrough striker Mark Viduka was the greatest ever Australian player. I thought he might say Harry Kewell, who was an absolute legend at Leeds.

It was at the end of the interview that I told him I knew about the bear hug and wanted to experience it for myself. As soon as I said it he gave me this look. He knew the pain he was about to put me through. I had no idea.

In fairness to him he was kind enough to warn me: 'I will give you one, but it's gonna hurt.' I thought 'Ah it'll be all right,' but he went for it and grabbed me in this hold that was so tight it felt like I would never get out. He squeezed the life out of me. I seriously had stars in my eyes, like I did when Hulk Hogan almost choked the life out of me.

Then he crunched me over and said: 'Normally I'd twist you round while lowering you and dumping you on the floor.' I was out of breath but managed: 'You've done enough, you've done enough.'

I really wish I hadn't asked. When he finally released me after the bear hug I was still seeing things. He was just laughing away and meanwhile I thought I was going to faint. I had to walk off camera.

EVERYONE LIKES A HUG, DON'T THEY?

I went to Chelsea that night and my back was still killing me. People were asking what was up with me: 'I asked for the bear hug from Mark Schwarzer and I shouldn't have.'

Looking back, it wasn't the brightest idea I've ever had. He's 6ft 5ins, an absolute mammoth and so strong, which is pretty impressive considering he is into his 40s. I was in agony.

I will never ask Mark Schwarzer for another bear hug, that's for sure. And I'll never challenge Sunderland midfielder Craig Gardner to show me a bit of boxing again either.

I met him and his brother Gary Gardner, who is at Aston Villa, at a boxing club in Birmingham that they were trying to help promote. It was a nice interview. But for some reason at the end I thought it would be a good idea to do a bit of boxing.

Once again it was not one of my brightest. I actually told them to show me their boxing faces and do a bit of shadow boxing. But Craig Gardner decided to actually proper lamp me in the stomach instead, catching me totally off guard. I tried to firm it in front of the cameras but he caught me good and left me with a bruise for a good two or three days. It didn't help that Gary Gardner followed that up with a dig as well. Craig Gardner still gives me stick about the day he had me on the ropes. He is feisty on the pitch too, as many Premier League players found out last season.

The low blows from the Gardner brothers should have taught me to always be alert, but the old Stoke long-throw merchant Rory Delap caught me out once again. They had just been battered 5–0 by Bolton a few days before

I met up with him, so I asked him what former Stoke boss Tony Pulis said afterwards.

He said he was quiet after the game and the players knew that eventually the hairdryer would come out when they saw him walk into the dressing room and he didn't say too much. At his worse, according to Rory Delap, Tony Pulis can 'fly off the handle and get pretty close to you, foaming at the mouth,' when the red mist comes down.

Obviously, I asked Rory to do an impression and show the world what Tony Pulis is like when he gets mad. At first he didn't seem keen, knocking me back every time I pestered him. I kept trying and trying but he wasn't biting. Maybe he feared another rollicking if he took the mickey out of Tony Pulis on TV.

Anyhow, he said no so many times I was convinced he wasn't going to do it, so I started preparing my next question. Then, out of nowhere he just launched at me, screaming and roaring at the top of his voice right in my face. Like the bear hug from Mark Schwarzer and choke hold from Hulk Hogan it came out of nowhere and shocked the hell out of me.

I was seeing stuff again. He could tell too. He even asked me if I was all right afterwards. I was certain he wasn't going to do it so it was totally unexpected. I imagine Fergie's hair-dryer treatment is something like that. It frightened the life out of me. He just went mad and then stopped as if he flicked the impression on and off with a switch. God knows what the real Tony Pulis is like in real life when he lets loose.

I loved interviewing Manchester City winger Scott Sinclair (he was at Swansea at the time) for two reasons.

One: there was no suffering involved, like with Mark Schwarzer, the Gardner brothers and Rory Delap. Two: he was happy to muck in and do anything we asked him, just for a laugh.

For some reason I thought he would be really quiet but he loved it and was more than happy acting and all sorts, and there was nothing he couldn't do. He really wasn't bad – maybe that's a future career idea for him, thanks to *Soccer AM*.

First up he played a receptionist at the Liberty Stadium. Then we took a trip up to the commentary box for Scott to describe one of his goals in his best commentary voice. He also showed off some decent dance moves in the dressing room and gave us a funny impression of Brendan Rodgers, his manager at the time, who is now at Liverpool. I like getting footballers to do impressions of their managers, to give supporters a tiny glimpse of what goes on behind closed doors. That's if the impression is any good, of course.

That was also the day that the boy band was started, the Liberty Jacks, featuring Fabio Borini, Ashley Williams, Scott Sinclair and Nathan Dyer.

It all started when Max went to Swansea to interview Brendan Rodgers and I was directing it. Some of the players came out to shout stuff at Brendan mid way through the interview. At one stage we caught all four of them stood up and leaning against a wall when we cut to them, looking just like a boy band. It was brilliant because I don't think they realised just how cheesy they looked until we worked our magic on the footage and put some boy band music and video special effects over it.

When I then got to sit down with Scott Sinclair it was time to start talking about getting the Liberty Jacks off the ground. Needless to say, they are still looking for a recording contract... a bit like myself! All in all he was a lovely bloke, Scott Sinclair. It is gutting to hear what has happened to him at Manchester City both with the move not working out and the serious injury he suffered. Hopefully once he returns from his loan spell at West Brom he can kick on again.

One of the funniest but weirdest things that a footballer has ever tried to take credit for doing to me is making me sweat. It sounds weird, but let me explain. I got an invite to Everton's training ground to interview the legend that is corner flag puncher Tim Cahill.

For starters we did it in a tiny room at Finch Farm and even though it was nearing the summer, for some reason I was wearing a big woolly jumper. At the same time I was also on the Atkins 'no carbs' diet (I had decided to give it a go to see if it worked, but I was also feeling pretty weak at the time). For some reason I was also sat on a heater that was pumping out a ridiculous amount of heat for the time of year. Now I think about it, I don't know why I didn't just say something in the first place and move. With the radiator blaring I started sweating up... . Apart from the jumper, Tim Cahill didn't know all the factors I was battling against and the conversation was going fine until it turned to Australian girls. 'Can you teach me anything about Australia?' he asked. 'It's got well fit girls,' I said.

That took us onto Holly Valance, the super fit Australian actress, singer and model. Unfortunately, at about the same time sweat started pouring down my forehead. Very quickly, and loads of it.

I was sitting facing Tim, with only the right side of my face in the camera. And as the sweat started to pour more and more I tried to slowly turn my face further away from the camera to hide my sweaty secret.

But Tim exposed me when even he couldn't keep a straight face any longer. 'Tubes I have to stop this. What's up with you?' he said, a little concerned, but mostly laughing.

'I'm sat on a radiator and it's boiling,' I explained.

Tim Cahill turned to the camera and said: 'I honestly can't concentrate because he's dripping. That's my claim to fame. I got Tubes talking about a topic that got him sweating. It was talking about the girls and Holly Valance. That's my claim to fame. I got Tubes all flustered!'

Once we stopped filming it was time to dry myself off and leave – but not without a little dig for Tim Cahill: 'Well, thanks very much for inviting me to this sauna.'

CHAPTER 18

DON'T BELIEVE
THE HYPE!

Even though being in and around footballers is nothing new, I am no different from the average football fan. I also make judgements about them and come to conclusions about what they are like without even actually knowing them. They are on our TVs or in the papers all the time, playing, speaking or doing something so often that eventually you feel like you know them.

One of the great things about my job, though, is being able to find out actually how close what I think is to the truth. So many players have been totally different to what I expected when I've interviewed them.

The interviews have probably also changed what many other people think about them too. For example, I know a lot of people think Michael Owen is boring, and I think a lot of people probably think that off the back of seeing him on serious programmes like *Match of the Day*. But how can you be funny on *Match of the Day*? It's not really the sort of programme you can go on and be really funny.

Anyhow, I can reveal, that the idea of Michael Owen being boring is 100 per cent not the case. He is actually a very funny man, with a real dry sense of humour.

It wasn't anything specific he did, it was just his general persona. He wasn't cracking loads of jokes. He was just taking the mickey a lot. I reckon a lot of people would have been surprised to see a really relaxed Michael Owen doing a running race with Helen at St George's Park when he gave us a tour.

The other thing that impressed me was how open he was and happy to talk about so many things that might be sensitive subjects. I asked him about the accusation that towards the end of his career he cared more about horse racing than football. 'I have written loads of articles about this on my blog,' he said, 'because I can't believe people give me the stick that I get about that.'

He also opened up about leaving Manchester United and revealed he actually phoned Liverpool and asked if he could come back. He said he would have done anything to go back. Just play a couple of games or even just hang around and coach the strikers. He really would have done anything to go back and finish his career at the club he started. But they said they weren't interested, which was a shame, and he went to Stoke instead.

Obviously he has now retired and I wish him all the best. After what he has done for this country I hope he stays in football and does well. I'll never forget seeing the Michael

Owen goal against Argentina in 1998 and being sat about four inches from the TV when he scored. I couldn't believe what I was seeing. What a goal. That is definitely one of my favourites.

Robbie Fowler – Haaa-lle-lu-jah! – another Liverpool legend, was the same as Michael Owen: a surprisingly and seriously funny guy. Fenners and I somehow got Robbie Fowler – Haaa-lle-lu-jah! – singing 'Lady in Red' when we met him at an advert we were filming. I know a lot of people also don't have him down as a funny guy, but that is definitely what we saw that day, when he was kissing Fenners and I, cheek to cheek, while singing 'Lady in Red'. Sometimes you have to step back and think: 'Hold on, that's a Liverpool legend!'

It reminded me of John Barnes when he came on the show and gave us a rendition of his 'World In Motion' rap from before the 1990 World Cup.

Phil Neville shocked me for different reasons. I thought he was going to be shy, quiet and not want to talk to me and Fenners. I had never seen him on TV or do an interview. And when he played football he never looked like the happiest of people (sorry Phil). But what a funny, funny man he is (even though he did annoy me by saying his favourite goal was against Chelsea). He was laughing at everything and dishing out the banter too, coming back at us whenever we piped up.

The cameraman mucked up once and Phil Neville was the first to start battering him. It was refreshing to see. It would be good to hang around with him and his brother Gary. Phil said his brother was his best mate in football and they are so close they speak every day; he was also the best man at Gary's wedding. I imagine Gary is quite a funny guy too. But I haven't met him yet, even though he works at Sky.

Phil Neville also told us a story about Paul Scholes and was raving about his vision and ability. 'His passing is ridiculous,' he said. He said he was sworn to secrecy and couldn't mention the name of the manager involved, but once a manager went to go for a number one in the bushes and Paul Scholes turned to Phil Neville and said: 'Watch this.' He then rolled the ball back, pinged it and it hit the unnamed manager straight on the head.

My first thought was: 'Was it Sir Alex Ferguson, was it Sir Alex Ferguson?' 'I can't tell you that,' Phil said. 'I just can't tell you who the manager was.' It can't be Sir Alex Ferguson. No way. I mean, who would be brave or mad enough to try a stunt like that?

Me and Fenners came out of the interview buzzing. 'How good was that,' I said.

It will be interesting to see what Phil Neville goes into now he's retired. I've been told he always wanted to be a lorry driver so I suppose that's an option. I wonder if he'll follow his brother into punditry. Gary Neville is a brilliant pundit, and I think Phil could follow in his footsteps.

In fact, Gary Neville is one of the best around, in my opinion, along with Graeme Souness. I love Graeme Souness's honesty. He is so straight to the point. I was really excited about meeting him once at Wembley Museum. He is a legend. But he is also known as being an absolutely tough as nails, so I can't pretend I wasn't a little bit frightened. But he was brilliant and did a bit of messing about with us.

I was bricking it before asking him to get involved with a bit of acting for the piece though: 'Graeme, there's a great, old skool picture of you in the museum with your big hair and your tache. Please don't knock me out for asking but...' He smiled and I thought 'I've broken him... '

'I'll be stood at the display cabinet and saying to myself, "Oooooh look at that rascal tache,"' I said. 'It doesn't need to be an Oscar-winning performance, but if you come up and pretend to have the hump with me it will look good.'

He thought about it for a few seconds then gave me a look, straight in the eyes that for a moment had me sweating... and then said: 'I'll do it.' Phew. That was a relief. I thought he was going to walk there and then and this story would have ended up in the chapter about interviews that have gone wrong.

Anyway, soon after, I was in acting mode standing at the cabinet with his photo in admiring his facial hair. 'Oooooh look at that rascal tache,' I said.

Graeme Souness marches over. 'What did you say?' he says with a stare that could kill to match the one from earlier.

'Er, er, er, nothing,' I said, whimpering like a little dog. 'Shall we go over there and have a chat?'

He was a really good laugh and a really interesting man, but I was scared because of his reputation. By the end of it I was buzzing because of the stories he was telling me from his playing and managing days.

He didn't quite finish the best one though – at one point

I was going to talk to him about Ali Dia, who he famously signed in 1996 when he was in charge of Southampton. He signed him after taking a phone call from someone pretending to be former World Player of the Year and AC Milan striker George Weah, who was recommending Ali Dia. It is quite an embarrassing story and I didn't think he would talk about it, but he actually brought it up so I asked him a bit more.

Then the soundman really annoyingly interrupted: 'Oh, can you ask that question again?' because a tannoy had gone off in the background.

But the interruption just gave Graeme Souness a chance to think about how much he actually didn't want to bring up that story again. 'Do we have to talk about that?' he said. I started trembling a little and was certainly not going to argue, so I just mumbled something back like: 'No Graeme. Not if you don't want to. No. No problem.' 'Good. Let's move on then,' he said. He was always winning that one.

It was the safest thing to do. And we sacked it off. I was really annoyed, but he is the sort of person who you tell before an interview: 'Anything you don't want me to ask you, or talk about, just say.'

Upsetting Graeme Souness is never going to end well. I have seen him around Sky since and he has given me the Graeme Souness nod, which I hope means I'm all right.

Kevin Keegan was another character I thought would be moody before I interviewed him. I still can't get his 'I would love it' retort to Sir Alex Ferguson out of my head. I think I based my opinion purely on that. But he turned up and was really happy, all happy and smiling and accommodating.

'Where do I need to be, what do I need to do?' – that is what he was like. I've seen him on other TV channels and I always think I don't know how to take this guy and have always got the impression that he wouldn't like being messed around.

I messed around – of course I did – but he took it well. He was filming a joke advert about passion and they made up an aftershave for the advert. He kept mentioning this spray during the interview and also spraying it all over me and in my face. At one stage he sprayed it in my eyes and I effectively went blind for a while. I genuinely couldn't see. Then I wrestled the bottle off him and started spraying him.

It was another 'did that really happen?' moment... Kevin Keegan and me, spraying each other with perfume?

He was talking about his relationship with Sir Alex Ferguson. He said they get on well and talk now, but back in the day they weren't the best of friends. But all the managers I have spoken to say Sir Alex Ferguson is just an immense man and they are privileged if they get an invite into his office for a glass of wine (including Owen Coyle, who is tee total, so didn't realise you don't put red wine in a fridge/freezer like he once did in Sir Alex's office).

After I came out of the interview with Kevin Keegan, I smelt as if I had come out of a brothel! On the way home I was on the train and everyone was walking past me and turning up their noses at the way I smelt. I can only apologise if you were one of those people. That smell was all Kevin Keegan's fault.

CHAPTER 19

TONGUE-TIED

Being a massive football fan, the chance to rub shoulders with some of the biggest players in the game should be a dream, right?

Well it is... except when it comes to meeting Chelsea players. Those situations tend to just turn into absolute nightmares for me.

You have probably guessed by now, if you didn't know already, that Chelsea are my team and Blue is the colour. But, to put it bluntly, whenever I see a Chelsea player I turn into a wreck.

I have done a few bits with the boys from the greatest club in the world, like collar them at the odd red-carpet event and a couple of teammates' interviews with Florent Malouda and the legend that is Frank Lampard. I've also asked John Terry, Frank Lampard, Ashley Cole, Didier

Drogba and Florent Malouda One Question and One Question Only.

The Ashley Cole, Didier Drogba and Frank Lampard episode was extra funny. They turned up at the PFA awards, breezed past all the media but stopped for me. A few people got upset that they ignored them but stopped to speak to me and *Soccer AM*... it was quite funny watching everyone get flustered. In fairness the players were late so they had to bypass all the media before they came over and said hello.

Once they were there in front of me I had to switch on pretty quickly to ask them a question. I obviously didn't switch on too much though. Think I asked them the best film or something irrelevant like that.

Ashley Cole gets a lot of stick, but I've always found him to be a really nice bloke. I know all the stories and have read about what he has done in certain relationships and I think what he wrote in his book about nearly crashing his car after hearing that Arsenal were only offering him £55,000 might have been a bit misinterpreted. But everyone makes mistakes. And every time I've met that guy he has come across as a top, top bloke.

He was always polite – and I might get caned for it – but every time I've met him he has been brilliant. It might be because we're from *Soccer AM* and it's a bit more fun, but he is always happy to come over and do bits and pieces for us.

The time I grew a pair to go and do Florent Malouda teammates, Helen decided to text John Terry and ask if I could also do One Question and One Question Only with him. John Terry agreed and said Ashley Cole was happy getting involved as well. Me and Big Ange, who I took as my rapping sidekick, were bricking it!

So when I had finished teammates with Florent Malouda, John Terry walked us through to the treatment room. To my surprise it was rammed with first team and youth team players. My heart was pumping hard I can tell you.

The time had come. Me and Big Ange delivered a mind-blowing rap (sort of) and John Terry and Ashley Cole had a good old chuckle, but before we could get the question out, Bill Blood, Chelsea's masseur, and the kit man started firing lyrics at us! The whole place went off, and to be fair their lyrics were mint. One of them was: 'You are Tubes, you've got man boobs.' I couldn't argue with that. I think I gave them one back and then it all ended.

Michael Ballack didn't know what the hell was going on. The look on his face said it all. I thought it was just going to be me and John Terry doing a question, but he had obviously told the staff and players to get involved and do something for us.

Bill Blood loved it. He is a real character, and often at the heart of the antics and jokes at Chelsea. Joe Cole said the funniest thing he's ever seen in football was Bill Blood getting picked up and lobbed through a wall by a couple of the lads, whose names, he said, would have to stay top secret. He said it was like a scene from a cartoon when a character gets chucked through a wall and all that you can see is the outline of their body.

As John Terry was driving out, he drove past us. He had played in the Champions League the night before and wound down his window.

'Tubes, you're Chelsea aren't you?' he asked.

'Yeah,' I said.

'Here you go , mate,' and he handed me his shirt from the night before, all signed and everything, and drove off.

The players wear different ones to the ones you can buy from the shops and he has his tailored, so the shirt he handed me was not one you can buy from the shop. That one is up on my wall at home.

Short situations like that are fine, especially if they funny. I can just muck around and that has never ever been a problem. But doing a serious interview with one of my heroes? That is a whole new kettle of fish.

I can handle sitting opposite a legend like Michael Owen with no fuss. Multi-award winning Hollywood actors? Easy. Big-name rappers? Won't even bat an eyelid. But Chelsea players? I am guaranteed to fold pretty much every time.

Because I watch Chelsea week-in-week-out and have grown up watching the likes of Frank Lampard and John Terry progress I have to pinch myself a bit. Like when John Terry was taking me and my brother around the training ground and introducing us to people. Just thinking about it now, it seems like a weird thing to even say, let alone do.

You would think over time I might man up over time and just get used to it. Especially as I live in Cobham and have bumped into Chelsea players loads of times because that is where their swanky training ground is. But, no, because I've been brought up a fan, they are still the only players who I see and clam up. The words get stuck in my throat and I get all starstruck. I must look and sound like a right idiot. Even more than normal!

It even happened when I had to speak to Dennis Wise on the phone. Helen – yet again – embarrassed me even more by asking about it when he came on the show and taking the mickey out of me for being so nervous when I was talking to him. He was cracking up.

It was during the week when I had to put in the research call. I've been doing these for years, so it really shouldn't have been a problem. Phoning Dennis Wise up I was petrified and trying to work out how to speak to him and what to say.

It should have got easier with Dennis Wise after that, but the next time was just as bad. I was doing a mickey take of the David Beckham pants advert, with the former manager and all round nice guy Harry Bassett, who lives near Dennis Wise. Dennis Wise came out of his house and drove past us. 'Oi Tubes, you all right, mate?' he shouted out the window. My response was a whimper. Still starstruck, and just wearing pants!

The worst was when I met the legend that is Frank Lampard in the pub and he came up to me. I was speechless. It was actually the second time I had bumped into him, but still my condition had not improved.

The very first time I met Frank Lampard was at a red-carpet event years ago. I called him over and said: 'Hi Frank I'm Tubes from *Soccer AM*.' He said: 'Yeah I know who you are.' And any words that I was trying to get out just wouldn't come out. I nearly fainted then as well! I had never met him before so had no idea he knew me.

The day I met him in my local pub I almost choked on my roast beef. I was trying to play it cool when I noticed he was there. My girlfriend at the time whispered to me 'that's Frank Lampard'. I was like a giddy, excited school kid inside, but trying to keep those feelings undercover as if I wasn't bothered at all. But I blew it when he came over. I was wolfing down a delightful Sunday lunch when I got the tap on the back. I spun round and staring back at me was the great man himself.

'How are you, mate?' he said.

I was fine, not that I could tell him as I clammed up and got tongue-tied. I'm sure I was saying something, but nothing was coming out. It was so cool that Frank Lampard was saying 'hello' to me. I was starstruck big time. You never expect Frank Lampard to pick you out in a pub full of people and say hello.

He wasn't drinking. He was in the pub watching the Manchester City v. Spurs game at the Etihad Stadium. It was a couple of seasons ago, when Jermain Defoe missed a big chance late on before Mario Balotelli won it with a penalty. And when they did it he reacted like a lot of people in the pub did that day: 'Ah, damn, they've done it!' Chelsea were well behind in the title race at the time, but a draw would have been the best result.

We ended up having a chat that day about Manchester City, Tottenham and just football in general. I just about managed to keep my cool but my heart was racing. Staying calm to do teammates with Frank Lampard was a little easier. I just put my professional head on and got the job done.

When I asked him who the slowest player was he started laughing and said: 'Well you're a Chelsea fan, you tell me.'

The first name into my head was Jon Obi Mikel and he started cracking up. 'Nah, nah, nah, he's actually quite quick,' he laughed before saying that he was actually the slowest, but that he has a couple of extra yards in his head. With 203 goals it doesn't really matter if you are slow though, does it? I'm slow – but I haven't got 203 Chelsea goals to my name, have I?

Frank Lampard came across as such a clever, grounded guy. And the fact he pulled Christine Bleakley and is getting married to her shows he is a true all-rounder. What a legend. I love the guy. Have you guessed?

Thank God Chelsea gave him another contract too because that would have been criminal if we hadn't. I could not believe the saga about his contract went on so long. Why would you not give a new contract to one of your greatest ever players? He has now broken Bobby Tambling's goal-scoring record and I think they've got to keep him at Chelsea for the rest of his life.

I grew up watching players like him, John Terry and Gianfranco Zola at Stamford Bridge, which is why I think I am so in awe of them when I meet them now. When I saw Gianfranco Zola on an Easyjet flight I realised just how bad things had got. I wonder if it's some sort of medical condition...

It was before the Man United v. Barcelona Champions League final in Rome. I was going out to Italy for my cousin's wedding and he was on the same flight heading to the final. On the plane was just me, my family, Gianfranco Zola, his wife and Man United fans. Loads of people were speaking to him, getting photos and things like that.

Everybody was saying to me: 'Go and have a word with him. You love him, he's your favourite player.' But I couldn't. Just couldn't. I was being a bit of weirdo. Just trying to listen to his conversation and hanging off his every word.

Since then I have met him. I wanted to cuddle him and just take him home (sounds weird, I know!) But I was way too scared to speak to him on the plane, even though I was probably his biggest fan.

When he was a Chelsea player I used to go to games and be in my seat a good hour before kick-off, sometimes feeling like the only person in the ground, just to watch him warm up. He used to kick the ball so high and then bring it down with the silkiest first touch. I then used to come home and try and copy it.

He's probably got quite a lot to do with my football career. My touch is probably the best part of my game and I would put that down to copying Zola in the garden. Kicking it as high as I can then trying to bring it down and do keep-ups. I even nicked one of his tricks that I spent ages trying to nail when you do keep-ups, but every time you make contact with the ball you swipe at it so it spins in the air. What a saddo, I know! But it was pretty handy when I used it in Skill Skool to beat Rocket.

The list of awkward encounters with Chelsea players is endless. The more I think about it, the more cringeworthy ones I can remember.

One of the most bizarre run-ins with the Chelsea boys happened a good few years back. Myself and one of my best mates, AJ, were sitting in his car waiting at a T-junction.

When I say car, what I really mean is a beaten-up Jaguar, which had graffiti all over it, as he had just completed the Scumball 3000 rally (I still have no idea what that is!). We were about to pull out at a junction and this massive white Ranger Rover with blacked-out windows drives passed us. 'Bet it's a footballer,' I said to AJ.

The car drove past and then reversed all the way back down the road, probably to double-check they really had seen the heap of junk they thought they had. I was confused and also a little worried because if a car pulled into the road while the massive white Ranger Rover was reversing back up it, it was a guaranteed crash.

The car stopped opposite us, the window goes down and sitting in it are Joe Cole, Damien Duff and Frank 'The Legend' Lampard. 'You all right Tubes?' Damien Duff said in his super-thick, extra-strong Irish accent. Once again I was bricking it. 'Er, all right. All right mate.'

It was all I could manage because, as well as being starstruck, I was hungover too. It was the day after Chelsea had won the league in 2006 when Joe Cole made Man United's defenders look silly and scored a worldy in a 3–0 win.

'You coming to arbar?' Damien Duff shouted through the window. I would have struggled to understand what he was saying at the best of times because of his accent... chuck in the stinking hangover I was nursing too? Not a chance. I didn't have a clue what he had just said.

He shouted it again. And again. It was getting awkward so I really needed to give him an answer.

In my head I was thinking: 'The harbour? Why would I

want to go there?' But despite the fact I didn't know what I was saying yes to I still mumbled back: 'Erm, erm, er, yeah. I might, erm, come down.'

'Why does he want us to go to the harbour?' I asked my mate. 'Where is the harbour around here?' What he was actually saying was the R Bar, in Esher in Surrey – though it took me about three hours to realise that and the fact I'd just been invited to Chelsea's title celebrations.

Joe Cole piped up too. 'You all right maaate. All right Pubes. Ha-ha-ha-ha-ha-ha. Come down, innit.' He still sounded really proud of himself for coming up with that nickname for me, did Joe Cole.

I remember when he christened me 'Pubes'. Him, John Terry and Eidur Gudjohnsen were in a pub in Esher which I was also in and they started texting 'We're with Pubes' to Tim.

If you want something to be kept quiet, Tim is one of the last people you want to know. So, unsurprisingly, for the next few weeks in the office everybody was coming up to me saying 'Morning, Pubes'. It's childish, but I love childish stuff. It makes me laugh.

I knew my nerves around Chelsea players were bad when I even did a runner from Paolo Ferreira. I walked into Cobham and Stoke D'Abernon train station and there was Paolo Ferreira waiting to get on the same train as me. Once again, I started bricking it, especially when he looked at me. And that was just for Paolo Ferreira. I didn't know what to say so I just ran up the other end of the train like a little school kid so I didn't have to talk to him.

At least I know I am far from alone when it comes to

suffering from this condition though. It helps to know there are others out there. My uncle Steve's girlfriend Susan also suffered from the Chelsea Chokes when she met – or should that say just stared at? – Didier Drogba at the Esso petrol station in Cobham.

It was a rainy day and she pulled in because she had a flat tyre. She was flapping about trying to get the pump out and all the bits to change the tyre. She got down on the ground to see to the tyre... then, all of a sudden, heard a booming voice behind her that said: 'Allow me.'

She is a massive Chelsea fan as well so was stunned to see that it was Didier Drogba. In the pouring rain, with no hesitation Didier Drogba takes over and changes the tyre for her complete with a fresh pump-up from the air machine.

Susan was in total awe. She managed to mumble a thank you, and even though he was absolutely drenched he just casually said 'No problem,' got back in his unreal car and sped off into the distance.

Now, if only I could be that cool when I meet Chelsea players.

CHAPTER 20

BLUE BLOOD

Quite literally, from the moment I entered the world I was a Chelsea fan. My late dad Brian got a teddy of Chelsea's mascot, Stamford the Lion, and put it next to me. Photo. Snap. Chelsea fan. Done.

My dad loved Chelsea and apparently not long after I was born my mum said 'You've got a kid now, Brian, and you can't neglect them for Chelsea.' His answer was 'I won't... I'll take him with me.'

He took me to my first game when I was four. It was Chelsea versus Watford. I was four years old, and freezing. He was feeding me Bovril and Wagon Wheels to shut me up. I was making such a fuss about being cold at that first game he was fuming. In the end we left early because I was making so much noise. He was not happy on the way home, I remember that.

I really had no choice who to support. My whole family are Chelsea.

I remember once there was a family barbecue and I was in my full kit (yep, full kit, wa...). I probably had shinpads on too and I managed to do 1,000 kick-ups. I had the whole family counting '1, 2, 3, 4,' all the way to 1,000 and when I got to the end my dad was beaming with pride.

'You see, that's Chelsea. That's what Chelsea have done for him.'

'No it's not,' I thought. 'That's what hours in the garden have done for me!'

I used to have a goal in the garden and play there every day with my mate until I totally messed the garden up. We used to have apple and pear trees there but we had them cut down so I could have a football pitch at the back. I used to get Gary, one of my best mates, round and put him in my Dmitri Kharine goalkeeper kit and stick him in goal just so I could score past him.

Now, it's just different. I sit in the Matthew Harding, which is brilliant. The atmosphere is great. There are certain areas of the ground that are buzzing and the noise is sometimes deafening; other sections at the bridge now are very quiet, which is a shame. Back in the day you would never have that. I suppose though that is what is happening with the game in general up and down the country because of the increasing prices of tickets etc. I still go and love it too though.

Things on the pitch are different nowadays too. The expectations have changed a little bit now to say the least. I don't mean to sound big headed but it's blooming great to be a rich club now. Back in the day when I would say I was a Chelsea fan, people would shrug their shoulders and just say 'oh, OK' – we were no threat back then so nobody was bothered. Now when I say I'm a Chelsea fan they always think it's because we've got loads of money and have won a few things in the last decade. Then I have to explain I've been going since eight and seen the years of no trophies and average players. But all I tend to get is 'yeah right ya just a glory hunter.' Which is frustrating, but you can't help it if a filthy rich Russian billionaire comes along and says he wants to buy your club. Which person or fan would say no to that?

I love it. I love the way things are now. Back in the old days we didn't expect to win. Anything. Now we go to finals or start the season and say 'we have to win' because we've got to be winning trophies. I think the crowds were more relaxed back in the day and would come up with funny chants, but now it is different.

But that's just the way football has evolved. That's life.

My best Chelsea memories? The 4–2 FA Cup game against Liverpool in 1997. I've never seen Stamford Bridge like it. We came back from 2–0 down to win 4–2. Gianluca Vialli got two and Mark Hughes and Gianfranco Zola scored. I actually thought the Matthew Harding Stand was going to fall down that day. It was a brilliant atmosphere and an amazing day.

One of the worst games was the Champions League final in Moscow against Manchester United in 2008. We did it in a day. Literally. We were up at 5 a.m. in the morning. It was a weird place, Moscow. When we lost after John Terry slipped and then Nicolas Anelka missed the final penalty, what happened after that rubbed it all in. The heavens opened and it started absolutely chucking it down.

Nobody told us what were supposed to be doing to get back to the airport and from the stadium and how we were supposed to get there. There was confusion everywhere and to top it all off we were absolutely soaked. We ended up just getting chucked on a bus, which they locked. The driver was behind iron bars so you couldn't get to him. It felt like we were going to prison.

We got to the airport and there were loads and loads and loads and loads of other buses. We thought the driver would just open the door and let us off, but for some reason he didn't. We were kept on the bus. Some guy was sick. Another guy passed out. Meanwhile the driver didn't give two hoots. It would've been all right if John Terry had scored that penalty and we were heading home as Champions of Europe. It wouldn't have mattered.

Then there was a free for all for the planes. Even Kerry Dixon got left behind. That's a Chelsea legend. That's how disorganised it was. Luckily super Uncle Steve is an absolute unit and sorted us out. He just bundled us all together and got us on a plane and screamed at someone: 'Where is this plane going to?' Fortunately they said Gatwick. People were so desperate to get out of there I heard stories about them ending up in Luton and elsewhere when they were supposed to be returning to other airports. Anywhere was better than Moscow.

Unfortunately, and I feel really bad about it, I missed the next occasion we reached a Champions League final in 2012. Typically, as I wasn't there, we won it.

I was sat at home watching it. I had to work in the morning and it was the day of the last *Soccer AM* show of the season. I was doing a performance and they needed me there. I looked into every possible option to see if there was any way I could leave at midday after the show and get to Munich in time for the final, but it was impossible. All the planes were booked. I even considered the Eurostar, going to France first and then onto Germany. But it was never going to happen. I tried so hard but failed.

At least we won. I was like a little kid again when Didier Drogba scored the winning penalty, running straight out into my garden doing laps and screaming my head off like an absolute nutter.

Who is my favourite Chelsea player of all-time? Gianfranco Zola. Closely followed by Frank Lampard, because that guy is 35 and still doing it. So impressive. He is amazing. And now Chelsea's highest goalscorer. And he is a midfielder. That is special.

I always think Gianfranco Zola is going to come back in some role at Chelsea. I'm convinced – he's doing well at Watford. Not sure if it will be as manager though. Now Jose Mourinho has come back I can see him staying for years and years and years now.

When Jose Mourinho first set foot in England and said 'I'm the Special One,' I raised my eyebrows and thought: 'Jeez this guy's confident!' You name me any other manager who has done that and then the same year basically proved it by winning the league and then loads of other trophies in the following seasons.

Now he is one person I would love to interview. There

were some whispers around *Soccer AM* towers about me going to Madrid to speak to him last season. I was buzzing at the thought. But until I was there in front of his face I had to take it with a pinch of salt.

Just as well I didn't get too excited as it didn't happen. But what a man, in my eyes he is the Special One! Just the way he conducts himself. If I could turn into a fly for a day I would go and listen to one of his team talks.

And I'd love to see a rollicking from Sir Alex Ferguson. Whenever I interview ex-Man United players I always try and get stories about Sir Alex Ferguson but they are just not interested. It's like talking about him is forbidden.

I remember interviewing Peter Schmeichel. He is a good talker and the sort I thought would give me a bit of juicy gossip. Even he wasn't having any of it. He wouldn't answer anything about him.

I asked Mikael Silvestre and Ryan Giggs what was the angriest they'd seen him, and they both pretty much did the same thing. Paused for a few seconds while they contemplated the question, before saying: 'The happiest... ' I cut both of them off: 'No, the angriest?' Both times all I heard was silence. So I would love to have seen Sir Alex Ferguson unleash the hairdryer for my own eyes.

As for Jose Mourinho, he knows everything off the top of his head. I have been told by some of the Chelsea players that whoever their opposition are, he has a profile on every single player. Strengths, weaknesses, favoured foot, heading ability, you name it, he knows it.

Joe Cole told me a story about him in an interview last season which sums this up. He said Jose Mourinho was the best manager he had ever worked for and probably ever would do. 'What's so good about him,' I asked, 'what does he do?'

Joe said: 'There was one time he walked into the changing room before a game at and he just turned to Paolo Ferreira and said: 'You will score today. You'll be on the right running into the box, the ball will come over, someone will flick it on and you will score.'

Joe Cole said he looked at John Terry and Frank Lampard confused, almost laughing because Paolo Ferreira never scores. 'Great player, Paulo,' he said 'but he never scores. Just like Claude Makalele.'

What happened in the game? Ball came over, flicked on and Paolo Ferreira scored. What are the chances of that? How did he know that? How can you predict someone is going to score like that? It was purely because he had done his homework on the opposition.

I would love to listen to what Jose Mourinho's got to say. I'd love to go for a pint with him, I reckon he's hilarious. And if I had to ask him One Question and One Question Only it would probably be: 'How do you know so much about football, considering you never played? You were a below average footballer but possibly one of the top five managers ever? You can't learn it from a book, so how have you got it?' That's quite a wide question so hopefully I could get a lot out of him.

I'm delighted he has come back. Just watching his first press conference on the day he returned, I was like a little kid. It's good for English football too, not just Chelsea.

It's a shame that Sir Alex Ferguson is not around any

more and has retired because the rivalry between them was good. I love all the pre-match talk that comes around before the big matches. They are massive friends but would both do anything for their team to win, which makes the papers great to read before all the big games.

I like to see how quick the managers are in their responses when they're being quizzed by journalists and how they bite back, especially as I have to do some of that in my own way. There was a classic from Jose Mourinho when he was unveiled and asked about accusations from Andres Iniesta that he had ruined Spanish football. His answer was brilliant and so quick – that he didn't ruin Spanish football, but he ruined Barcelona by ending their dominance and winning this that and the other.

I love to see how quick people are and at the same time how people fold under pressure. Like Rafa Benitez did when he made his 'Fact' retort to Sir Alex Ferguson all those years ago when he was Liverpool manager. It makes football like a soap opera.

And I love that the king of the banter, Jose Mourinho is back on his throne Chelsea's future should be healthy now he is back. I think he will stay for a good seven or eight years and we will do big things. Within six months of him being there I reckon players who were on the brink of big things will be world beaters – players like Eden Hazard.

I hope we are patient with our young, English players too now. I mentioned Scott Sinclair earlier. I wish he was still at Chelsea. In my opinion he is better than Florent Malouda and Salamon Kalou when they were there. Josh McEachran looks like he could be another who goes down the same path. He has been out on loan a lot in the last couple of seasons, but they should just keep him there and train him up. Let them look at and learn from Frank Lampard. You don't have to send these players away where they get forgotten.

But it's good to see Ryan Bertrand break through. It gives the youngsters there a bit of hope. Nathaniel Chalobah is another one who is a big hope and had a great season at Watford last year. Hopefully Jose Mourinho will look at these kids and give them a chance.

Of course, he will spend money. I'm convinced it will be great. All the changing of managers at Chelsea down the years is one of the side effects of Roman's money. Obviously I went to every game, but it's a bit tiring when you know a manager is only going to be there for a while and it won't be long before it is all change again. But now I'm buzzing again. And I think a lot of Chelsea fans will think now Mourinho's back.

And, without wanting to sound too much like the big man himself, it feels like the family is back together. I can't wait.

TUBES EXTRAS

TUBES'S TARGETS

To play for Chelsea... OK I'll settle with scoring a goal at Stamford Bridge.

To meet and cuddle Mila Kunis.

Try to get James Bond (Daniel Craig) to speak to me or even sit in the same room as me... he hates me!

Collaborate with Jay Z, Snoop Dogg (or Lion, or whatever animal he calls himself by the time this is released) and, of course, Vanilla Ice.

To not go completely bald (Wayne, I might need your help pal).

Interview Jose Mourinho.

To rekindle my love affair with Alesha Dixon (I'll give in to her constant text messages sooner or later).

See England win the World Cup in Brazil... my gosh I love a Brazilian.

Lose the moobs (sorry ladies, I know they really get you going).

To become best friends with Gianfranco Zola.

To get Slash to like mash.

Give Steve Coogan a one-inch punch.

TUBES EXTRAS

TEAMMATES

Quickest interview: Noel Gallagher. It basically went like this: 'All right Noel?' 'I'm good thanks Tubes. That was your question, now seeya!' I felt like a right doughnut. Luckily the great man let me ask my question, which was: 'When you start losing your hair will you shave it off, or wear a wig?' His answer was 'Shave it off'!

Slowest interview: there have been quite a few slow/long ones, including Denzel Washington and Jim Carrey, but I'd probably have to say the American actor from *The Hangover*, Bradley Cooper. He must've asked me about four or five times if I was going to punch him! So most of the time was taken up by me reassuring him that I wasn't.

Hardman: interviewed many hardnuts – Jason Statham, Tamer Hassan, Danny Dyer, Dolph Lundgren, Hulk Hogan, The Rock and Ray Winstone – but I'd have to say Sylvester Stallone! For an 85-year-old he's in tip-top condition... Rocky, what a lege... Adriaaaaan!

Most skilful: probably the wrestler John Cena. He freestyled a two-minute rap on the spot and absolutely put me in my place! Also the genius that is Dynamo the magician. That bloke is mustard! He runs Paul Daniels pretty close, ha-ha. Now that's magic!

Best dancer: over the years I've had the pleasure of cutting shapes with many people. The ones who have the sickest moves are Gerard Butler, Bacary Sagna, Colin Salmon and Peter Crouch. There has to be one winner though... Blake Harrison, who plays Neil from *The Inbetweeners*. I've never seen moves like it! Pure class.

Worst dancer: I can claim that one! I've got no rhythm whatsoever and the only time I hit the dance floor is after a couple of stiff morale-boosting drinks! So every year when the dance-off comes around I'm in all sorts of pain, mentally and physically! To this day I have never won it. Not even Joe Hart's dance that I copied helped me last time around. Came second though, so thank you Joe!

Worst dressed: has to be Keith Lemon, as for half the interview he was topless... as was I! We shared and compared our moobs (I won), Kelly Brook (fit as, I would like to point out) was not impressed. Sorry Kelly.

Joker: I've met loads of people with loads of banter, Colin Farrell and Will Ferrell have to be up there, but I would have to say Denzel Washington just takes the title for me. It was totally unexpected. He played along and basically just mucked around for five minutes after I got told he was a moody man and that he would hate me!

Most intelligent: probably Sir Ben Kingsley. What an absolute legend that man is. One of the best actors ever (and he watches *Soccer AM*). My favourite scene in a film ever is when he is playing Don in the film *Sexy Beast* and he is giving it large to Ray Winstone. 'Grosvenor Friday you'll be there, yes yesyesyesyesyesyesyesyesyes, No nonononononononono.' Genius of a man.

Most fazed: don't get me wrong she's an absolute stunner, but it has to be Jesssica Alba. She just didn't get what I was doing (mind you, half the time neither do I!).

Most attractive: Wowser! – this is a tough one. I've had the pleasure of meeting some absolute fitties – Carmen Electra, Alesha Dixon, Eva Mendes, Jessica Alba, to name but a few – but my favourite has to be Jessica Biel. She is an absolute sort and legs eleven. Also her banter is second to none. Justin Timberlake, you are one lucky man, what have you got that I haven't? Oh yeah, everything.

Rudest: by far Steve 'I love myself' Coogan. Don't think I have or ever will meet a fella like him. Don't see the point of going through life being like that.

Longest in the shower: got to be honest. I get on quite well with the people I meet, but not that well to have a shower with them. Saying that some of the ladies I've met over the years I wouldn't mind having a shower with oi oi...

TUBES EXTRAS

WHY I LOVE FOOTBALL

My earliest memories of football are... going to watch the mighty Chelsea when I was four. My first game was Chelsea v. Watford and it was freezing! I was piping up complaining that I was cold, but my dad just gave me a Wagon Wheel and a cup of Bovril and told me to shut it. I carried on moaning so we had to leave early. The old man was fuming! Sorry Dad.

My footballing hero is... the little genius that is Gianfranco Zola, I have never seen anyone with a better touch. What a magician he was. I used to get to Stamford Bridge early on match days just to watch him warm up! Then I would go home and spend hours in the garden doing kick ups and copying the tricks he was doing. It was probably down to him that I hold the FATV kick-ups record. Thanks Franco.

My favourite ground is... of course, the mighty Stamford Bridge. All this talk about moving ground worries me. Stamford Bridge is Chelsea's home and it should stay that way. I used to love standing in the Shed end... oh the good old days. The atmosphere in the Shed was mega. I now have a season ticket in the Matthew Harding upper. Come on the Chels!

My favourite thing about match day is... having a little sing-song with my fellow Chelsea fans. My favourite song has to be 'Ten Men Went to Mow' – as it gets nearer reaching 'ten' the Matthew Harding is rocking! To this day I don't why I taught Jim Carrey the Celery song! He enjoyed it though, ha-ha.

The greatest game I've ever watched is... there are two if that's all right? Okay, thank you. Chelsea v. Bayern Munich, Champions League final! Beating the Germans in their own back yard was mega. How we managed to win the Champions League that year I'll never know. The other game has to be Chelsea 4–2 Liverpool in the FA Cup back in 1997. We were 2–0 down at half time and quite frankly getting our botties slapped. We ended up winning 4–2 (big thanks to supersub Mark Hughes who changed the game). And we went on to win the cup that year... happy days.

WHY I LOVE FOOTBALL

My favourite piece of memorabilia is... I would probably have to say a Chelsea shirt signed by the legend that is Frank Lampard. What a man, what a player... Super Frank. I also have a pair of signed Gianfranco Zola boots he used to wear for training. They are so small it's frightening.

You wouldn't know I used to... be a cleaner, and a very bad one! How I ever kept that job I'll never know. I was pathetic. Mr Muscle would have been ashamed.

If I hadn't had football growing up I would... have been massively bored and maybe a better cleaner? Actually, probably not. Even now when the football season ends I'm begging for it to return sharpish!

If I could change anything I would... completely scrap that doughnut they call the 'fifth official', who stands behind the goal! Can someone please tell me what they actually do? Yeah, that's right... nothing. Also clubs that play music after they have scored a goal, what is all that about?

Football fans are great because... the majority of them are proper funny. Some of the songs and comments they come up with are priceless! Also I love that one fan who's had one too many pre-match beers and spends the whole game trying to get everyone to sing! Classic.

I love football because... it's the best game that has ever been invented, it brings people together and life without it the world would be a sad, sad place. One Question and One

TUBESOLOGY

Question Only... if you put 100 blokes in a room and said you couldn't talk about football or girls then what on earth would you talk about?